Scotland at War

1. The balloon goes up: barrage balloons in the River Forth.

> "I don't know why but I always thought barrage balloons looked like giant silver elephants in the sky. It certainly gave me a sense of security to see them over the Clyde."
>
> *Former Clydebank Resident*

SCOTLAND AT WAR

Ian Nimmo

Archive Publications Ltd

in association with

Scotsman Publications Ltd

First published 1989 by

Archive Publications Ltd
10 Seymour Court
Manor Park
Runcorn
Cheshire
WA7 1SY

in association with

The Scotsman Publications Ltd
North Bridge
Edinburgh 1

ISBN 0-948946-53-9

Printed in Europe

BIBLIOGRAPHY

Calder, Angus: *The People's War*
Chamberlain, E R: *Life in Wartime Britain*
Churchill W S: *The Second World War*
Gilchrist, Donald: *Castle Commando*
Harris, Paul: *Aberdeen at War; Glasgow at War*
Hume and Moss: *Glasgow at War*
Kerridge, Roy: *People of Britain*
Kochan, Miriam: *Britain's Internees in the Second World War*
Historical Sources for Central Scotland: World War Two
HMSO: *Front Line 1940 - 41; The Official Story of Civil Defence of Britain*
Johnstone, B S: *The Evacuees*
Jones, R V: *Most Secret War*
Lewis, Peter: *A People's War*
Lovat, Lord: extract and information taken from *The Weekly Scotsman 1960*
Macphail, I M M: *The Clydebank Blitz*

Newspaper files: *The Scotsman; The Evening News;* the *Weekly Scotsman;* the *Glasgow Herald, The Stirling Observer; The Press and Journal; Evening Press*
Firemen at War: *The story of the NFS and AFS in Scotland*
ARP Guide: *Edinburgh*

> "Mr Chamberlain's broadcast telling us that we were in a state of war with Germany was not too impressive as I recollect it. Sounded too much like an apology. Another war was the last thing we wanted, yet somehow there was relief that all the uncertainty was over. Somebody just had to do something about Hitler. I reasoned that if I volunteered for the Seaforths I had a better chance of getting into them than waiting to be called up and taking the chance of being sent to an English regiment. My father had been with the Seaforths in the First World War. I volunteered next day and that was it."
>
> *Inverness Pensioner*

Contents

Acknowledgements

Many people have assisted in the research for this book, particularly in the search for pictures of Scotland during the war years, and I would like to thank the following for their ready help: the staffs of the National Library of Scotland; Edinburgh Central Library; The Mitchell Library in Glasgow; the Imperial War Museum, London; The Museum of Flight, East Fortune; Huntly House Museum, Edinburgh; the People's Palace Museum, Glasgow; Clydebank Library; The Scotsman Publications library, printing and editorial staffs; Mr Ian McMurtrie, of Lothian and Borders Fire Service, for opening the picture file and wartime memories to me; the library of D C Thomson and Co Ltd, Dundee and its staff, and the company's helpfulness in giving me access to it; The Fine Art Society Ltd, Edinburgh; Paul Harris for access to his own war picture file and for his general helpfulness and expert knowledge.

I would also like to thank members of the four small reminiscence groups I formed, some of whom were too shy at the time to allow attribution. To preserve their privacy in this respect I happily agreed to publish all their names but without direct identification and I am therefore indebted to Margaret Barker, Joyce Clements, Margaret Gibson, Susan Imrie, Fiona Murdoch, Jean McCallam, Jessie Nolan, Elizabeth Robertson, Tom Davies, John Ferguson, John Kirk, David McDiarmid, Jack Menzies, Colin Paterson, Ian Paterson, James Reston and many others who have at one time or another passed on their wartime stories to me. Thank you all.

IAN NIMMO
AUGUST 1989

The Eve of War

On the day war was declared lightning struck Scotland twice in the same place. For some people it was a matter of passing interest only; for others it was a talking point as they recognised a remarkable occurrence. Those who were on Greenock's Princes Pier during that worst thunderstorm for many years certainly felt lucky still to be alive. But on that historic Sunday of 3 September 1939, as Britain held its breath in anticipation of impending conflict, some also saw it as an omen. With Germany again on a war footing and memories still vivid from the last encounter, it was inevitably seen by some as a bad omen, either for the Clyde or for the country.

The countdown to that last weekend of peace had gripped the country in uncertainty for years. Yet only twelve months earlier, on 30 September 1938, Prime Minister Neville Chamberlain had been hailed as a hero when it seemed that he had miraculously averted the looming holocaust of a second great war within two decades. Britain had watched with increasing concern the growth in Germany of the Nationalist Socialist Party under Hitler. Their ideological doctrines, their political opportunism and their lust for power and European domination were signs that presaged only one outcome. German re-armament, conscription, the annexation of Austria, the warring rhetoric and the mounting demands which could not be appeased all confirmed that the only way Hitler might be stopped was by confrontation. When Hitler turned his attentions to Czechoslovakia and prepared for a pre-emptive strike — ostensibly to defend that country's German-speaking minority — the grim realities of war stared Britain again in the face.

Hysteria had accompanied the onset of World War One; now Britain surveyed the Czech crisis with cold reluctance. It was clear our country did not want war, but inexorably we were being sucked into it. As the tensions mounted, gas masks were issued, trenches dug, new wills were signed by the thousand and food and petrol were hoarded. For the vast majority of the British public the prospect of another war was appalling. "How horrible, fantastic and incredible it is that we should be digging trenches and trying on gas masks here because of a quarrel in a far away country between people of whom we know nothing" said Chamberlain, signalling to all that the sell-out of Czechoslovakia was

---

We, the German Führer and Chancellor and the British Prime Minister, have had a further meeting today and are agreed in recognising that the question of Anglo-German relations is of the first importance for the two countries and for Europe.

We regard the agreement signed last night and the Anglo-German Naval Agreement as symbolic of the desire of our two peoples never to go to war with one another again.

We are resolved that the method of consultation shall be the method adopted to deal with any other questions that may concern our two countries, and we are determined to continue our efforts to remove possible sources of difference and thus to contribute to assure the peace of Europe.

[signature]

Neville Chamberlain

September 30, 1938.

4. The Munich Declaration of September 1938 and the outbreak of war is delayed - but not ultimately avoided.

THE CORPORATION OF GLASGOW
EDUCATION DEPARTMENT.

EDUCATION OFFICES,
129 BATH STREET,
GLASGOW, C.2.
March, 1939.

TO THE PARENTS OR GUARDIANS
OF CHILDREN IN GLASGOW.

DEAR SIR (MADAM),

Evacuation of Children from Glasgow in the Event of a National Emergency.

It will already be known to you that the Government are making plans to enable parents who live in the crowded areas of large cities to have their children transferred to safer places if war should ever break out.

The city of Glasgow is included in the plans, and all parents in Glasgow, particularly those who live in the crowded parts of the city, will want to consider whether their children should be included in the arrangements

Under the arrangements which are being made the children would gather at the primary school nearest their home and the older and younger members of each family would as far as possible be evacuated together. They would go to the chosen places in the care of teachers who would remain with them. They would live in the country in houses where they would be welcome. Arrangements would be made to let you know their new addresses as quickly as possible. Children under school age would also be allowed to go if the mother or a woman friend went with them, and all the children of one family would be sent to the same place.

In any case, I have to ask you to show on the attached form whether or not you would wish your children to be included in the scheme. This question is being put to you now, so that the Government may be able to complete, in peace time, their plans for the evacuation of children from this city, if, unfortunately, war should break out.

I am,

Yours faithfully,

R.M. Allardyce

Evacuation Officer.

5. By the beginning of 1939 the authorities had plans well in hand which could be implemented upon the outbreak of war.

6. *above:* Shortly before the outbreak of war, the 2nd Btn, The Cameronians.

8. *below:* The Scots Guards prepare for war: a bren gun mounted on an anti-aircraft tripod.

7. 2nd Btn, The Cameronians.

9. *above:* Tea for King's Own Scottish Borderers.

10. *below:* King's Own Scottish Borderers limbering up for war.

preferable in his view to Britain's involvement.

With such tensions it was hardly surprising that Chamberlain's eleventh-hour dash to Munich and his confidence that the discussion with the German Führer had ensured "peace in our time" brought widespread relief. At home he was met by an ecstatic throng of 20,000 on his return to Heston airport. There were shouts of "God bless you, Neville" and group-singing of "For He's a Jolly Good Fellow". The police for a time could hardly contain the excited multitude, such was the public euphoria that the country was not going to war. Cabinet Ministers, who had prayed for the success of his mission, came to the airport along with thousands of flag-waving children to demonstrate their appreciation. Then there was that dramatic moment when the Prime Minister held up the fateful document which bore the signed pledges of both himself and Herr Hitler and read from it:

"We regard the agreement signed last night and the Anglo-German Naval Agreement as symbolic of the desire of our two peoples never to go to war with one another again.

"We are resolved that the method of consultation shall be the method adopted to deal with any other questions that may concern our two countries, and we are determined to continue our efforts to remove possible sources of difference and thus to contribute to the assurance of peace in Europe."

Lord Halifax, the Foreign Secretary, handed Chamberlain a personal letter from the King. The Canadian Premier sent a congratulatory telegram which spoke of unbounded admiration for the service which Chamberlain had rendered mankind. "On the very brink of chaos", wrote Mr Mackenzie King, "with passions flaming and armies marching, the voice of reason has found a way out of the conflict which no people in their heart desired but none seemed able to avert."

It was the understandable, heady, thankful relief of someone who had witnessed what had seemed to be the unattainable. The world may indeed have been peopled by sceptics as far as Hitler's intentions were concerned, but for those few hours at least, before the doubts began to re-assert themselves, a nation resigned to war grasped frantically at the slender hope that it could be avoided.

There was only one resignation from the Government, that of Duff Cooper, but thirty Conservatives, led by Churchill, abstained from voting when the settlement was debated in the Commons. "The highwayman", growled Churchill referring to Hitler, "had demanded a pound and grudgingly taken 18s 6d and the rest in a promissory note."

In the end, as the world now knows, Munich made war a certainty. Herr Hitler's visions, his policies of insatiable German expansion, power and dominance had to be challenged. One short year later, in September 1939, the passions were again flaming and the armies marching as Poland became Hitler's next target. Although this country still longed hopefully for peace, it was falling over the precipice — a fact recognised by all, it seemed, except the Prime Minister.

On that first and last September weekend of peace, Scotland tried to forget the apprehension and think of other things. The sunny skies and soaring temperatures seemed to add to the general incredulity. Some pretence of normality

11. The French battleship *Dunkerque* in the Forth, 10 June 1939.

had to be made, and the crowds turned out on the Saturday, as usual, to watch a full soccer programme. With the season just five games under way, Rangers led the First Division with a hard-won victory over Third Lanark at Cathkin Park. "Gerry Dawson was worth a medal in the Rangers goal", declared one sports writer mindful of war-like references; he went on to report that a young man called Willie Waddell was demonstrating promising form on the right flank, while team-mate Willie Thornton, another later Ibrox hero, was bang on target with a fierce shot and finished among the scorers. Twenty thousand supporters roared on their favourites after youthful defender Willie Woodburn arrived late for the kick-off due to traffic problems — the result of something to do with a possible war, he said.

Over at the Paradise John Divers beat three players before giving Celtic a 1-0 win against Clyde. Hearts beat Motherwell 4-2 and Hibs lost to Albion Rovers 3-5. Aberdeen were fourth in the First Division, Dundee were top of the Second Division. A wag at Muirton Park, where Aberdeen were comprehensively beaten 3-0, noticed the military connotation, and disconsolately remarked that as far as he was concerned the entire Dons team could be given a free transfer to the Highland Division. There were teams on view that last Saturday that no longer exist (although not all of them were casualties of the war) like Edinburgh City, King's Park, St Bernards and Leith Athletic. On that last peacetime Saturday they at least provided ninety minutes of war-free thought.

It was felt, however, that because of the unstable situation the St Leger should be abandoned; but the tournament committee of the Craw's Nest Tassie decided with commendable spirit that golf was not going to be interrupted by Mr Hitler if they could help it. The tournament would therefore jolly well go on at Carnoustie as planned. It was the weekend Marguerite Wilson broke the women's cycling record from Land's End to John o' Groats, and set a new time for 1,000 miles of one day, seven hours and thirty minutes. Walter Hagen announced he had decided to retire 'slowly' from golf after making around £200,000 from the game.

On that eve-of-war Saturday, cinema-goers were queuing throughout Scotland to see James Stewart and Carole Lombard in *Made for Each Other*, while John Wayne was providing "one smashing climax after another" in the all-time great Western *Stagecoach*. Heavy firing was heard from all fronts as Harry Carey starred in *Law West of Tombstone* and Tyrone Power and Henry Fonda were the good baddies in *Jesse James*. Bing Crosby was in fine voice in *East Side of Heaven* and Laurel and Hardy had them rolling in the aisles in *Blotto* while Eddie Cantor made his audience forget the present for a chuckle in *Roman Scandals*. The pulling power of the silver screen was at its height as it purveyed instant escapism from the stark realities of recession and uneasy peace. Edinburgh boasted thirty picture houses at that time, and at one of them was a film reflecting the sinister forces ranging against the country — showing at Pooles Roxy was Robert Donat and Madeleine Carrol in *The Thirty-Nine Steps*.

On that last weekend of peace you could buy a fashionable lady's felt hat for 12s 11d, a double bed for 22s 6d, a gent's raincoat for 16s 9d, a sound vest and pants for 2s, a Blackbird pen for 7s 6d, a packet of ten Kensita cigarettes for 6d, a watch for ten bob, a Simcett Silver Cross Pedigree pram with ball-bearing wheels from £2 2s, or you could sail from Glasgow to New York for £22. Steel Coulston was

12. The Royal Scots Greys on exercise, 1938.

13. Dundee schoolchildren go through a gas mask drill.

proclaimed Britain's best beer, Usher's was "man's hope" and Grant's Standfast was the "best whisky in any measure". A new Vauxhall 12hp saloon was £150 and a 1936 Lanchester or Wolsley were bargains at £85 and £75 respectively. More to the point, you could buy a fire extinguisher for 21s and a torch for indoor use during the blackout for 9d.

On that last weekend of peace the numbers of convicted persons sent to prison in August were 24 in Edinburgh and 167 in Glasgow. In the Capital the official figures were down on the previous year, up in Glasgow. There was a total of 463 people throughout Scotland jailed for non-payment of fines, which was an improvement on the previous year. Church ministers were kept busy as hundreds of young couples, anticipating possible separation, decided to marry in a rush, and toy manufacturers had a final fling at the tills as toy tin helmets flooded the shops. But Uncle Mac — Donald McCulloch of the BBC's *Children's Hour* — preserved a state of quiet calm among the little ones, ably supported by Dennis the Dachshund, Larry the Lamb, Auntie Doris, Auntie Muriel and Romany as the BBC went on to its own wartime footing.

On that last Saturday, accepting that a peace miracle would not occur twice and that life might never be quite the same again, the BBC issued the following statement: "You are asked to adjust your sets to a wavelength of 391 metres or 449 metres — that is to say, the wavelengths of Scottish Regional or North Region. Broadcasting throughout the United Kingdom will, until further notice, be confined to these two wavelengths. Meanwhile, all stations of the BBC are closing down. Until further notice a single programme without alternatives will be broadcast continuously on these two wavelengths only, from 7 am to 12.15 midnight." In the background the censor was sharpening his scissors and red pencils in readiness to ensure that only information which was in wartime public interest would be broadcast or published in newspapers.

The nation had every reason to fear the worst. After Munich, Herr Hitler's demands had become no less shrill. The trusted process of meaningful consultation to avoid war, symbolised in Chamberlain's 'piece of paper', was proved worthless. Hitler was forcing Europe over the edge and British involvement was unavoidable. Chamberlain, the 1938 hero of the hour, was suddenly perceived as an ineffective and even naïve old man. Irrespective of his sincerity and good intentions, the country's harsh judgement of him was that he was a failed peacemonger confronting a fanatic whose megalomaniac demands were incapable of satisfaction. It became painfully apparent that Chamberlain

14. Dundee schoolchildren from Craigentinny School, Edinburgh, are evacuated at the beginning of September 1939.

15. Mothers and children evacuated from Glasgow on the steps of Haddo House, Aberdeenshire.

was the wrong man, in the wrong place, at the wrong time in history. He was the arch appeaser. Hitler was not to be appeased.

In the early hours of 1 September 1939, less than six months after stating that he had no further territorial aims, Hitler ordered the German battleship *Schleswig-Holstein* to open fire on Polish fortifications at Westerplatte and his *Wehrmacht* troops crossed into Poland. This time his designs were on the port of Danzig, a Free City under a League of Nations mandate. A non-aggression pact with Russia had caught the rest of the world by surprise and paved the way for the German *blitzkrieg* — lightning war — that hurled a million troops in six armoured and eight motorised divisions over the Polish border. By 6 am Warsaw was being bombed. The courageous Poles were crushed; 60,000 died, 700,000 were prisoners. Poland had gone.

Sensing that this was the trigger to full-scale war in Europe yet reluctant to face the truth, Britain and France, who had guaranteed the Polish frontiers, made a final attempt at a negotiated withdrawal of Hitler's armies. It was futile. Chamberlain was on the rack, a man in torment. His instinct was still to conciliate, to delay making that awful, final decision. In the end it was his own Cabinet which took the lead and forced his hand, and Chamberlain sent his ultimatum to Hitler to suspend his attack on Poland. The expiry time was 11 am on 3 September.

The country waited in suspense for Hitler's response. There was no panic, no passion, no fuming, no tears. During these last few hours of peace it was a time for private thoughts and personal preparation. Many people stayed at home waiting for the Prime Minister's broadcast. Those who went to church were assured that their ministers would relay the message to them from the pulpit.

At 11.15 am on that quiet Sunday morning, speaking in solemn but firm tones, the Prime Minister addressed the nation on BBC radio. This is what he said in full:

"I am speaking to you from the Cabinet room at No 10 Downing Street. This morning the British Ambassador in Berlin handed the German Government an official note stating that, unless we heard from them by 11 o'clock that

16. Evacuees leave Dundee East Station, 2 September 1939.

17. Evacuees at a Deeside school.

they were prepared at once to withdraw their troops from Poland, a state of war would exist between us. I have to tell you now that no such undertaking has been received and that, consequently, this country is at war with Germany.

"You can imagine what a bitter blow it is to me that all my long struggle to win peace has failed. Yet I cannot believe there is anything more, or anything different, that I could have done that would have been more successful. Up to the very last it would have been quite possible to have arranged a peaceful and honourable settlement between Germany and Poland. But Hitler would have none of it. He had evidently made up his mind to attack Poland whatever happened, and although he now says he put forward reasonable proposals which were rejected by the Poles, that is not a true statement. The proposals were never shown to the Poles, nor to us, and although they were announced in a German broadcast on Thursday night, Hitler did not wait to hear comments on them but ordered his troops to cross the Polish frontiers the next morning. His action shows convincingly that there is no chance of expecting that this man would ever give up his practice of using force to gain his will. He can only be stopped by force, and we and France are today, in fulfilment of our obligations, going to the aid of Poland, who is so bravely resisting this unprovoked attack upon her people.

"We have a clear conscience. We have done all that any country could do to establish peace. The situation — in which no word given by Germany's ruler could be trusted, and no people or country could feel itself safe — had become

intolerable, and now we have resolved to finish it. I know you will all play your parts with calmness and courage. At such a moment as this the assurances we have received from the Empire are profound encouragement to us.

"After I have finished speaking, certain details will be announced of the plans the Government have made, and I ask you to give them your close attention. The Government have made plans under which it will be possible to carry on the work of the nation in the days of stress and strain that may be ahead. But these plans need your help. You may be taking your part in the fighting services or as a volunteer in one of the branches of civil defence. If so, you will report for duty in accordance with the instructions you have received. You may be engaged in work essential to the prosecution of the war or the maintenance of the life of the people — in factories, in transport, in public utility concerns, or in the supply of other necessaries of life. If so, it is important that you should carry on with your jobs.

"Now, may God bless you all. May He defend the right. It is the evil things that we shall be fighting against — brute force, bad faith, injustice, oppression and persecution — and against them I am certain that the right will prevail."

On the Western Front Hitler was addressing his troops. As long as the German people were united, he said, Germany would not be conquered. It was lack of unity in 1918 that had led to collapse. Whoever offended against this unity need expect nothing else but annihilation as an enemy of the nation.

Hitler told the *Wehrmacht* that once again England was

pursuing a policy of German encirclement. "I have many times offered England and the English people peace, the understanding and the friendship of the German people", he stressed. "My whole policy was based on the idea of this understanding. I have always been repelled by England."

In Scotland the report of Hitler's speech in the morning papers brought wry comments that, reluctant though we were to go to war, someone really had to teach Adolf the difference between England and Scotland.

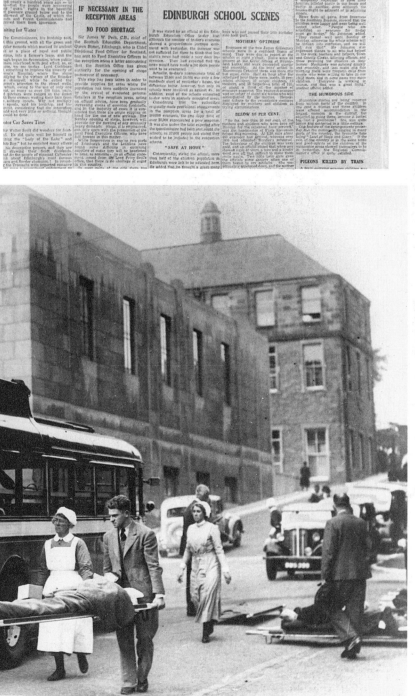

19. Patients are evacuated from Edinburgh Royal Infirmary in anticipation of massive casualties immediately upon the outbreak of war.

20. Mobilisation and recruits to the Argyll and Sutherland Highlanders are trained in the use of bayonets for expected trench warfare, September 1939.

BRITAIN ORDERS COMPLETE MOBILISATION

King Signs Orders at Privy Council Meeting

The German Onslaught

TOWNS BOMBED

Many Casualties in Warsaw

GERMAN ATTACKS "ON ALL FRONTIERS"

Reich Navy "Takes Over" the Baltic

TREATY INVOKED

Poland Asks Britain for Her Aid

A.R.P. WARNINGS IN OPERATION

Mobilisation and "State of Siege" in France

THE DAY'S EVENTS IN BRIEF

KEEP CALM

STATE THE LORD PROVOST AND TREASURER

LONDON SAYS POLAND JUSTIFIED

THE PRIVY COUNCIL

KING SIGNS VITAL ORDERS

MEETING LASTS ONLY 12 MINUTES

PARLIAMENT TO MEET TO-NIGHT

Cabinet Session

MEDIATION OFFER

FRANCE REPLIES TO DUCE'S PROPOSAL

Edinburgh Evening News

ONE PENNY.   SUNDAY, SEPTEMBER   1939   SPECIAL EDITION

BRITAIN AT WAR

Premier Tells The Nation By Radio

The nation first learned that it was at War with Germany in a broadcast by the Prime Minister at 11.15 a.m. Mr Chamberlain said:

"I am speaking to you from the Cabinet Room at 10 Downing Street.

"This morning the British Ambassador in Berlin handed the German Government an official note stating that unless we heard from them by eleven o'clock that they were prepared at once to withdraw their troops from Poland a state o fwar would exist between us.

"I have t otell you that no such undertaking was been received, and that consequently this country is at war with Germany.

"You can imagine what a bitter blow it is to me that all my long struggle to win peace has failed.

"Yet I cannot believe that there is anythong more or anything different that I could have don that would have been more successful.

"Up to the very last it would have been quite possible to have arranged a peaceful and honourable settlement between Germany and Poland, but Hitler would not have it.

"He had evidently made up his mind to attack Poland whatever happened, and, although he now says he put forward reasonable proposals which were rejected by the Poles, it is not a true statement.

"The proposals were never shown to the Poles nor to us, and Hitler did not wait to hear comments on them, but ordered his troops though thy fere announced in a German broadcast on Thursday night to cross the Polish frontier.

"His action shows convincingly that there is no chance of expecting that this man would ever give up his practice of using force to gain his will.

"He can only be stopped by force, and we and France are to-day, in furfilment of our obligations, going to the aid of Poland, who is so bravely resisting this unprovoked attack upon her people.

"We have a clear conscience. We have done all any country could do to establish peaec.

"The situatilon, in which no word given by Germany's ruler could be trusted, and no people or country could feel itself safe, had become intolerable, and now we have resolved to finish it.

"I know you will all play your parts with calmness and courage.

"At such a moment ais this the assurance which we have received from the Empire are of profound encouragement to us.

The Prime Minister went on to say that the Government had to carry on the work of the ination in the days of stress tha tlay ahead, and he appealed to all who were required for service to report for duty in acordance with their instructions.

The Prime Minister concluded: "Now, May God bless you all. May we defend the right. It is evil things that we shall be fighting against, brute force, bad faith, injustice, oppression, and persecution, and against them I am certain that the right will prevail."

MUSSOLINI'S ELEVENTH-HOUR EFFORTS

A Rome message says that Italian diplomacy, under the guidance of Signor Mussolini, worked all night in an effort to formulate a last attempt to preserve peace.

Count Ciano, the Italian Foreign Minister, is understood to have had a long conference with Signor Mussolini immediately after the British and French Ambassadors, Sir Percy Loraine and M. Francois Poncet, had visited Count Ciano yesterday evening.

United States plans for the mobilisation of industry have already attained a scope equal to that of the third year of the Great War.

POLAND'S LOSSES

In an interview with a Reuter representative, the Polish Ambassador in London, Count Raczinski, made a statement this morning regarding the attitude of the Polish Government towards the Italian proposal for a Five-Power conference.

He said: "As long as a single enemy soldier stands on Polish soil, so long will any talk of conferences remain ludicrous and fantastic.

"Moreover, the fact of German aggression has introduced a complete change in the situation. Thousands of lives were lost, of whom a very high percentage were civilians, in bombed towns and villages.

"The material losses are already very considerable, and demand full reparation."

IN DOWNING STREET

A GRIM AND SILENT CROWD

Ministerial activity in Downing Street began early to-day, despite the midnight meeting of the Cabinet.

Departmental officials were still going on duty when Sir Thomas Inskip entered the Dominions Office at 9.3 5a.m. Four minutes later Sir Kingsley Wood, the Minister for Air, accompanied by Sir Edward Campbell, arrived by taxi, and Sir Kingsley entered 10 Downing Street. The announcement of Britain's ultimatum to Germany was the signal for intense excitement in Downing Street. Within 24 minutes the whole of the south side of the street was packed by men and women, who had hurried to the scene to watch the arrival of Ministers.

Mr Greenwood called at No. 10, and remained there nearly half an hour. Shortly after his arrival, Sir Archibald Sinclair called at No. 11, and later Sir Samuel Hoare arrived, and with Captain Margesson, Chief Government Whip, entered the Chief Whip's office.

PREPARED

An air of tense expectancy marked the crowd while peace and war were hanging in the balance. Not even a hum of conversation broke the silence. All faces were turned towards No. 10. There were grim faces, old faces, and young faces, but written on them all was a spirit of preparedness for whatever eleven o'clock might bring.

At 10.40 Sir Samuel Hoare left No. 10 and walked to the Foreign Office.

It was evident from the deserted nature of the streets that in Edinburgh most people were either at church or in their homes listening to the announcement by the Prime Minister. In Princes Street, immediately after the declaration, the scene was one of peace, the sun shining brightly and persons making their way to places of worship.

Some cheering was heard from down in the valley in the Gardens. They came from a trainload of soldiers which was slowly pulling out of the Waverley Station.

This quiet loveliness, however, about half an hour later was disturbed by the screaming of air raid sirens, and the city knew without any doubt that we were at war. Even so, there were no signs of panic. Some people could be seen sitting in the Gardens, and they never moved from their seats. Other people continued strolling along the main thoroughfare and adjacent streets, while on the Waverley Bridge a couple of small boys who were larking about never stopped in their play.

WHERE THE WINDSORS WILL STAY

When the Duke and Duchess of Windsor arrive in Britain they will stay with Major E. D. and Lady Alexandra Metcalfe, at Colemans Hatch, in Ashdown Forest.

Major Metcalfe is an old friend of the Duke of Windsor, and was best man at his wedding.

Red rear lamps, hooded and dimmed so that no light is thrown directly upwards and no appreciable light is thrown on the ground, are now obligatory on all pedal cyclists between sunset and sunrise.

WORLD NEWS IN SNAPS

A Proclamation was issued at Canberra to-day calling out for war Service members of the Naval, Military, Air, and Civil Defence forces.

The Tokio "Yomiuri Shimbun" declares: "Britain's firmness must have surprised Germany, who though that armed blackmail would bring acceptance of her demands.

The Viceroy, Lord Linlithgow, has asked Mr Gandhi to visit him and consult with him on the opinion of Congress.

The German Minister in Helsingfors visited the Finnish Foreign Minister yesterday, and informed him that Germany would respect Finland's neutrality.

The German Government has passed a decree empowering confiscation of wireless sets capable of picking up foreign stations.

The Polish liner Pilsudski is safe in a European port, according to a wireless report from Warsaw. The liner left New York for Gydnia several days ago.

NEUTRALITY OF EIRE

DECLARATION BY MR DE VALERA

A declaration that Eire would remain neutral was made by Mr De Valera to the Dail yesterday when emergency laws were passed giving the Government absolute powers. The Premier went on to say that Eire would take measures to protect herself and maintain trade with Britain, but Ireland's history and the fact of the partition of Northern territory made neutrality the only course.

Senator Sir John Keane said that the large majority in Ireland was in sympathy with the democracies in the crisis and if Britain was not unfriendly it would do more to unite Ireland than anything else.

Senator Frank Macdermott said that if Britain, France, and Poland were defeated, everything spiritual that the Irish race held dear would be defeated too. They would go down to oblivion and destruction.

"LAST DROP OF BLOOD"

POLISH DEPUTIES' RESISTANCE PLEDGE

Polish deputies of all parties, including Ukrainians and Jews, pledged their "last drop of blood" for Poland, in a special session of the Sejm Chamber, in Warsaw.

The pledge was given after the Prime Minister, General Sladow-Skladowski, had made an appeal for national unity. The session was kept secret for fear of air raids.

HEAVY VEHICLES

WIDE. CHANCES IN DRIVING REGULATIONS

The Ministry of Transport has issued emergency orders in connection with the use of goods transport motor vehicles, extending the scope under which lorries and vans may be used.

Region Traffic Commissioners are empowered to permit any person to act as heavy goods or public service vehicle drivers or as conductors of public service vehicles for 12 months from the date of the permit.

Further regulations allow variations of existing road public services, authorising temporary services and also new routes. Owners can use any vehicle whether it has an A, B, or C licence, and other vehicles not licensed can be taken into the scheme.

Evacuation of Regent's Park Zoo has gone off without a hitch. All the rarer animals have been sent to Whipsnade. Among them are Tang, the male giant panda, and Ming, the young giant panda.

The 29 members of the Australian Rugby team reached Plymouth yesterday. Dr Matthews, the team manager, said, "I cannot say what will happen. We are entirely in the hands of the English Rugby Union."

The Railway Executive Committee give notice that consequent on the present emergency the return halves of tickets issued for any period of more than one day which would normally expire in September, will be available for use on any train until the end of that month.

22. The historic special edition of the Edinburgh *Evening News,* published on Sunday 3 September 1939.

THE 18-40 MEN

Calling Up Process Will Be Gradual

No Difference Between Married and Single

Mr Brown, who was moving the first reading of the National Service (Armed Forces) Bill, said that the object of the Bill was to make all fit British subjects, aged 18 and 40 inclusive, liable to be called up for service with the armed forces of the Crown during the war emergency.

"The Bill," he said, "does not in general place liability on those fellow-citizens to be called up for service, but provides for proclamations to be issued from time to time. By this means it will be possible to issue proclamations as and when they are required, making various age groups liable to be called up for service.

"It is not intended at the outset that any considerable number of men other than those already liable shall be called up. Steps will be taken to ensure that man-power essential to industry shall not be taken away."

MINISTERS EXEMPT

Men required for service would be required to register and would be medically examined and receive their enlistment notices. The procedure for these purposes would be similar to that which had been applied in respect of Militiamen under the Military Training Act.

A new clause had been added providing that any citizen in Holy Orders or a regular minister in any religious denomination was exempt.

The Bill did not apply to Northern Ireland or the Isle of Man, but there was power to extend it to the Isle of Man by Order-in-Council.

There was provision for postponement of service on the ground of exceptional hardship.

CONSCIENTIOUS OBJECTORS

The clause dealing with conscientious objectors was almost identical with that of the Military Training Act.

There was another proposal which was not in the Act. It had been found that there were very few conscientious objectors—at the moment he only knew of three—who had refused to register for conscience or to apply to a tribunal.

The Bill therefore provided that in cases of this kind the Minister might, if he had ground for believing the man was a conscientious objector, provisionally register him on the register of conscientious objectors, and refer his case to the appropriate tribunal. This would obviate the difficulty of such men being placed on the military register to begin with.

Provisions for reinstatement in employment had been included in the Bill. It was felt that what had been the practice of good employers should continue to receive the sanction of the House.

"The present Bill," Mr Brown said, "marks a major departure in our national policy, and, backed as it will be by this House, will show the world what we mean in this emergency."

LABOUR'S VIEW

LOWER AGE LIMIT SHOULD BE 20

Mr Arthur Greenwood said that he was still an anti-conscriptionist at heart, and he did not suppose that his attitude would ever change, but since the last Act was passed an entirely new situation had been created.

"We have decided," he added amid cheers, "if a second reading be challenged in the Lobby, to support the second reading of the Bill.

"We are somewhat disturbed at the extension of the Bill to youths from 18 to 20. We should have preferred that the Government kept its original conscript age of 20 and worked up, if need be, about the 40 mark."

Mr Greenwood asked the Government to give earnest consideration to this point.

MAXIMUM EFFECT

"I believe," he continued, "that it must be made clear to our Allies, and more especially to Poland, and to all nations friendly and unfriendly, that the whole of our human and material resources will be thrown behind those who are the victims of aggression.

"This is no time for cheap heroics, for talking about fighting to the last man and the last penny, but it must be made known to the world that we do not enter lightly upon an undertaking of this kind, and that when we do we must do it fully and completely."

It might be that we would not need all the men who might be brought under the Act, but the essential thing was that our resources both in men and materials should be properly organised to secure the maximum effect.

"There will be as vital work at home as there may be overseas," said Mr Greenwood. "There will be as vital work in dungarees as in uniform."

NO PROFITEERING THIS TIME

He asked that profiteering should be stopped, and, amid cheers, declared: "He who seeks personal gain in these times is a traitor to his country. We will not tolerate the creation of war fortunes this time.

"As far as possible, we should pay as we go along, rather than leave a crushing and intolerable burden of debt to be borne by an impoverished people who will have to face the largest problem of reconstruction ever to be faced in our history.

"We must conserve our resources as far as possible, and, if need be, we must go short of many things now. Every effort should be made to control prices of the essentials of life.

"It would be unforgivable if early and more effective steps are not taken to keep the cost of living as reasonable as possible.

"We shall support the Bill in the conviction not merely that it may be needed at some future date, but in the conviction that it may bring encouragement and a new spirit to those to-day who are facing the bombs of the dictators."

MR MAXTON OPPOSES

Sir Percy Harris (Bethnal Green, Lib.) agreed that private individuals should not be allowed to exploit the national need, with the enemy almost at our gates. This Bill must go through its stages as rapidly as possible. While the Bill would be approached in a non-party spirit, he hoped every Member would see that when it became an Act it should not unfairly discriminate between the duty and responsibility placed on every household in the land.

Mr Maxton (Glasgow, Bridgeton, I.L.P.) said that he and his friends opposed the measure. The Government would not be doing the right thing by the people of this country as a whole unless some corresponding measure was very speedily introduced to deal with property along parellel lines with the way in which it was proposed to deal with human life.

"This is not merely military conscription," he said. "It is industrial conscription also. For every man of 18 to 41 this decides where he is going to be and where he is going to serve."

BOYS UNDER 20

LADY ASTOR WANTS THEM TO STAY AT HOME

Mr Wedgwood (Newcastle-under-Lyme, Lab.) suggested that the situation was not so dangerous as it had been painted from countless platforms and in the Press.

"I have bet an even fiver with my friend Mr Stokes, the Member for Ipswich, that there will not be a bomb dropped on London in the next six months, and I am certainly not inclined to hedge that bet."

This war was likely to last a long time—it might be a decade, and success would depend not solely on the organisation of the Forces but on the continuation of our financial soundness and on our export trade.

In the long run we would have one advantage over Germany, in that we could, thanks to the British Fleet, carry on our trade. It was important in this struggle to carry on business as usual with a firm upper lip without too much interference with trade and without too much sandbagging and A.R.P.

WARNING TO ENEMIES

Major Milner (Leeds, Lab.) said: "I feel that the Bill is essential for the successful prosecution of the project on which we are about to embark. It is essential to ensure fairness between man and man as a gesture to our friends in other countries, as a warning to our enemies, and as a concrete indication of our determination to see this matter through."

Lady Astor (Plymouth, C.) asked the Government, if possible, not to send boys under 20 to the front.

"I am not doing it from the point of view of my own boys," she said, "because they are over 21, but it does really have a psychological effect, and even if they get well it affects them for life.

"For the good of the country, for the good of the Army, and for the future, I do hope, if it is possible, that we shall be able to keep the boys under 20 at home, and I am sure it will be the wish of the whole country."

MOST VIGOROUS MANHOOD

Mr Hore-Belisha, Minister for War, said it was the intention to call up classes of age groups in an orderly manner.

"We have selected a range of ages between 18 and 41, representing the most vigorous manhood of the nation," he said, "but it does not follow, from the fact that we have begun at the age of 18 for the purpose of this Bill, that we intend to call up that class as the initial class."

Mr Hore-Belisha added: "The Military Training Act falls to the ground, and is replaced by this Bill before the House."

Questioned whether there was to be any differentiation between married and single persons, Mr Hore-Belisha replied: "No, sir, unless exceptional hardships exist."

ADVICE TO MOTHERS

MR TOM JOHNSTON, M.P., ON EVACUATION

BILLETING OF FAMILIES

"Administrative difficulties created by a number of mothers in reception areas is the only trouble we have encountered so far," said Mr Thomas Johnston, M.P., at the office of the Regional Commissioner for the Scottish Civil Defence Region, Palmerston Place, Edinburgh, when interviewed by an "Evening News" reporter this forenoon. Mr Johnston said that mothers who were arriving with large families had sometimes expressed reluctance to allow the children to be divided up, even for a temporary period.

"NO CONFUSION"

Naturally, the local authorities had a very limited number of houses where they could put, say, seven of one family into, and occasionally there was some difficulty in getting suitable accommodation for them as one unit. He wished to impress upon the mothers before they go that it might be necessary even as a temporary expedient to have their families billeted partly in one house and partly in another, even although the houses might be adjacent or in adjoining streets.

News from all parts, from Inverness to the Southern Borders, showed that the children were happy and were being well looked after. "People who are scheduled as evacuees for to-day must go to-day," Mr Johnston added. "They cannot wait until Sunday or Monday, otherwise the whole scheme will be thrown into confusion, and we will not risk that." Mr Johnston also expressed thanks to all who had helped in the work, teachers and helpers, Town and County Clerks, billeting officers, and those receiving the children in their homes. Machinery was running quickly and smoothly, and last night and this morning there were frequent calls from people who were willing to take in one child more, and in some cases two more children. "Everyone is working in unison, and that was a great thing," another official added.

THE HUMOROUS SIDE

Humorous stories are being reported from various parts of the country. In one case a woman and three children were offered accommodation in the largest mansion in the district, but objected to going there, because it looked too like a poorhouse! She was quite happy and contented in a little cottage.

One feature of the arrangements yesterday was the community singing in many parts of the country, the favourite tune being "Land of Hope and Glory." If the rest of the country is in the same fettle and good spirits as the children of the vulnerable areas showed themselves to be in yesterday, the Regional Commissioner's office is quite satisfied.

EDINBURGH A.R.P. PERSONNEL

Chief Constable W. B. R. Morren, who is in charge of the A.R.P. organisation in Edinburgh, stated last evening that all paid A.R.P. workers who were available had been called out, and other voluntary workers were being absorbed for shifts of duty as required. Some of the A.R.P. workers had been on duty since Thursday night, and the matter of arranging suitable hours for all members was now the principal problem which faced them.

DAMAGE TO ESSENTIAL BUILDINGS

Government Loans for Repairs

To ensure the repair of essential buildings damaged in war, the Government will grant loans either through the local housing authority or the appropriate Minister. There will be no repayment of capital or payment of interest during the emergency.

This does not concern housing accommodation.

The arrangements will apply to buildings which in the opinion of the appropriate Minister (a) are essential to the welfare of the civil population; (b) have become wholly or partly incapable of use by reason of war damage; (c) can be repaired at a reasonable cost; and (d) whose repair is essential owing to the lack of similar buildings available.

The buildings are divided into three categories: (a) Buildings owned or occupied by local authorities, e.g., hospitals, first-aid posts, schools; (b) buildings of the same class, but in private ownership; (c) buildings not directly connected with the normal activities of a local authority."

PRIVATE PROPERTY

For buildings owned or occupied by local authorities the appropriate Minister may direct repairs to be carried out, lending the necessary money.

As regards privately owned buildings, if the owner is financially unable to have the repairs done, the housing authority may be required either to lend the money or do the repairs.

For buildings coming into the third category the housing authority or the appropriate Minister may lend the necessary money.

The appropriate Minister may lend money for the reinstatement of plant when conditions are satisfied.

HOUSING CONTROL

EVICTIONS BY COURT ORDER ONLY

The Rent and Mortgage Interest Restrictions Bill presented in the House of Commons last night provides that in war-time all houses previously decontrolled and new houses built since April 2, 1919, with rateable value up to £90 in Scotland, shall be controlled. It also provides that no mortgage be called in if the interest is paid regularly.

Houses belonging to housing authorities are excepted. The control will be that of the existing Rent Acts.

So long as the tenant pays the legal rent and otherwise complies with the requirements of his tenancy he cannot be evicted without leave of the Courts—which will not be given except in very exceptional circumstances unless there is suitable alternative accommodation. Similarly, a mortgage cannot be called in so long as the interest is paid punctually, and the existing rate of mortgage interest cannot be increased. Houses belonging to housing authorities are excluded.

DEBT RECOVERY IN WAR

NO ENFORCEMENT OF PAYMENT ORDERS

The new Courts (Emergency Powers) Bill applies to Scotland.

Under the first clause no one may, without the Court's leave, proceed to execution on any Court order for payment or recovery of money. There are certain exceptions. Proceedings are not to be started for fore-closure or for sale in lieu, and action is not to be taken in any such proceedings begun before operation of the measure. No one is to exercise any remedy available to him by levying distress, taking possession of property, or appointment of receiver of property, re-entry upon land, realisation of securities or forfeiture of deposits, or the serving of demands under Paragraph 1 of Section 169 of the Companies Act, 1929.

This is not to apply to proceedings available following default in debt payment, or the performance of obligations, or debts arising under contracts made after operation of the present measure has begun.

Where a bankruptcy or winding-up petition has been presented, and the debtor or company proves the inability to pay is due to war, the Court may stay proceedings under the petition.

VOICE OF EMPIRE

"One Flag, One King, One Cause"

Three Dominions Give Their Pledge

MR R. G. MENZIES, THE AUSTRALIAN PRIME MINISTER, DECLARED TO-DAY: "WE STAND WITH BRITAIN."

"THE BRITISH CABINET," HE SAID, "HAS MADE A MOMENTOUS DECISION. UNLESS GERMANY WITHDRAWS FROM HER ATTACK ON POLAND, BRITAIN WILL TAKE UP ARMS TO HONOUR A GUARANTEE SOLEMNLY GIVEN TO DEFEND CIVILISED MAN FROM THE EVIL DOCTRINES OF BRUTALITY AND LAWLESSNESS.

"We do not yet realise what the price in terms of human life and happiness will be, but we know that the British nations throughout the world are at one.

"There is unity in the Empire ranks—one King, one flag, one cause. We stand with Britain."

MUNITION FACTORIES READY

After a meeting of the Australian Executive Council a proclamation was issued early this morning declaring "a danger of war." It was signed by Sir Winston Dugan, Governor-General of Victoria, deputising for Lord Gowrie, the Commonwealth Governor-General.

In a broadcast address, Mr Menzies declared that "war could only come if Germany wanted it."

Australian munition factories are ready for instant and full production, according to an announcement by Mr R. G. Casey, Minister of Supply and Development.

"SHOULDER TO SHOULDER"

Sir Earle Page, former Commonwealth Prime Minister and Leader of the Country Party, has pledged the support of his party to the Commonwealth and United Kingdom Governments.

Mr Dunstan, Premier of Victoria, has promised Victoria co-operation.

Melbourne streets throughout last night were practically deserted. The people were all at home listening-in to Mr Menzies' broadcast and the latest news bulletins from Europe.

The papers to-day declare that Britain and France have no option after the "final act of barbarism in bombing defenceless cities."

"Australia stands shoulder to shoulder with Britain against the fanatic," says the "Sun." The "Argus" writes: "The Motherland and her daughters are united in the determination to end the rule of the lawless."

CANADA'S MESSAGE

EFFECTIVE CO-OPERATION WITH BRITAIN

Canada will be at the side of Britain. This was stated in a message from Mr Mackenzie King, the Canadian Prime Minister, which Mr Chamberlain received to-day.

It stated: "Following a meeting of the Cabinet this morning, a proclamation was issued summoning Parliament to meet at the earliest possible date, September 7. The following statement of Government policy was issued to the Press at one o'clock to-day:

"'In the event of the United Kingdom becoming engaged in war in the effort to resist aggression, the Government of Canada have unanimously decided, as soon as Parliament meets, to seek its authority for effective co-operation by Canada at the side of Britain.'"

FORCES ON ACTIVE SERVICE

"Meanwhile, necessary measures will continue to be taken for the defence of Canada. Consultations with the United Kingdom will continue in the light of all the information at its disposal.

"The Government will recommend to Parliament the measures which it believes to be the most effective for co-operation and defence. The Government has provided for the immediate issue of a proclamation under the War Measures Act, in view of the existence of a state of apprehended war.

"The Militia of Canada, which a few days ago was called for voluntary service under Section 63 of the Militia Act, has, under Section 64 of the same Act, been placed on active service. The naval services and the Air Force have also been placed on active service."

A plan to give thousands of British children a haven in Canada in the event of air raids on the British Isles is being submitted to the Canadian Cabinet by the organisation "Voluntary Registration of Canadian Women."

THE NEUTRALS

EIGHT STATE THEIR ATTITUDE

ITALY'S DECLARATION TANTAMOUNT TO NEUTRALITY

Eight European States have declared their neutrality. They are Denmark, Finland, Iceland, Norway, Sweden, Latvia, Estonia, and Portugal.

Authoritative Fascist circles in Rome consider the Italian Cabinet's declaration that "Italy will not take any initiative in military operations" to be tantamount to a declaration of strict neutrality.

Italy, these circles state, has made every effort to reach a peaceful solution of the present crisis. Italy's best contribution now is to help to circumscribe the conflict by not joining in.

U.S. POSITION

In the United States President Roosevelt told reporters that he believed that the United States could keep out of a European war. The administration would make every effort to keep out.

Late last night it was reported from Washington that, while it was too early to say that a swing over in neutrality sentiment was already pronounced, undoubtedly a movement in that direction was beginning.

In Tokio all indications point to Japanese neutrality. The "Hochi Shimbun" declares: "By the conclusion of the non-aggression pact between Germany and the Soviet Union Japan has been exempted from the obligation of supporting Germany if a second world war breaks out."

THE NORTHERN COUNTRIES

The governments of the Northern countries have simultaneously published declarations proclaiming their absolute neutrality in the war.

It is stated that the stipulations regarding neutrality enumerated in the declaration made on May 27, 1938, by Denmark, Finland, Iceland, Norway, and Sweden will come into force. This declaration affirmed the desirability of ensuring that the rules adopted by each country to govern their conduct towards belligerents should be similar.

M. Hansson, the Swedish Prime Minister, broadcasting last night, expressed his horror at the calamity which had come upon the human race, already tormented enough. It was necessary, the Premier said, for every Swede to play his part in keeping the country out of war. Tens of thousands of young men would be called to the colours for the strengthening of the defence of the country. The Prime Minister said Sweden's food supply was good.

NO DECISION BY SPAIN

The international situation was discussed at a long meeting of the Spanish Cabinet at Burgos last night. No official intimation was given as to whether Spain would remain neutral. The communique merely stated that the Government "examined the grave situation created in Eastern Europe," and that "it continues to follow with the greatest attention the course of developments at every moment."

The Government at Lisbon stated officially to-day that Portugal would be neutral.

"In such a grave moment, we would not retract from our alliance with Britain," stated the proclamation. "Happily it does not call upon us in moments of emergency to abandon our neutrality."

The Hungarian Government is withholding any declaration of neutrality, as it does not recognise that a state of warfare exists at present.

THE CABINET

Possibility of Four New Ministers

But No Labour Members

A POLITICAL CORRESPONDENT LEARNS THAT THE CABINET HAS BEEN WIDENED. MOST PROBABLY FOUR NEW MINISTERS WILL BE INCLUDED, AND IT IS ALMOST CERTAIN THAT MR WINSTON CHURCHILL IS AMONG THEM.

In order to facilitate the transition from a peace to a war administration all the Ministers put themselves unreservedly in the hands of Mr Chamberlain yesterday. They took this course with a single desire to help the formation of a Government on a broader basis such as that which came into existence shortly after the declaration of war in August 1914.

The Prime Minister has for a considerable time contemplated some such step in case an emergency should arise.

CHURCHILL AND EDEN

Amongst Ministerialists, and even amongst some who are ordinarily in Opposition to the Government, the inclusion of Mr Winston Churchill and Mr Eden has long been advocated.

It is believed that in considering the changes that are expected, Mr Chamberlain has adopted this view. It is also believed that he desired the return of the Liberal colleagues who went out of office on the adoption of the tariff system after the crisis of 1931, and it is thought that Lord Samuel and Sir Archibald Sinclair have been invited to join the Government.

Mr Chamberlain is understood also to desire to incorporate in the Ministry some members of the Labour Party who are now in Opposition.

LABOUR'S DECISION

Members of the Labour opposition will not join the reconstituted Government.

This decision was reached at the meeting of the National Executive in London to-day, which lasted nearly four hours.

It is understood that the decision has been communicated to the Prime Minister.

The decision does not involve any difference with the Government in its resistence to aggression. The party has already declared that it is prepared fully to back the Government in its policy of resisting aggression in Europe.

NEW SHELTER

FOR EDINBURGH BAC[...]

MORE EVACUATION URGED

The offer of co-operation with the Local Authority from the Edinburgh Trades and Labour Council was yesterday submitted to a meeting of Edinburgh A.R.P. Executive, when a deputation was received consisting of Councillor Mrs Ingles, Mr Wightman, and Mr W. P. Earsman, the secretary.

Mr Earsman pledged the wholehearted support of the Labour organisation. As an earnest of this it was suggested that Labour should be represented on the various special committees created by the Local Authority at this time.

Mr Earsman was assured by the chairman, Councillor Falconer, Chief Air Warden, that the Town Council had this in view.

The deputation also asked for further days to be allotted to evacuation purposes. They offered to co-operate in conducting meetings in the various congested districts for the purpose of stimulating further movement of the population from the city.

SATISFACTORY PROGRESS

The Evacuation Officer, Mr J. B. Frizell, indicated briefly the position at this stage. He explained that the movement of evacuees from the city was continuing, and up to date over 30,000 of the population had been successfully transferred. He regarded this as particularly satisfactory, having in view the various difficulties—human, economic, and otherwise—which presented themselves to those who might be in a position to go away from Edinburgh.

Mr Frizell undertook to bring the suggestions of the deputation before the

Department of Health, which is the Government department responsible for directing evacuation policy, and which would be reviewing the situation shortly.

The deputation referred to several other matters, all of which are to receive further and active consideration from the Executive. Councillor Falconer, on behalf of the Lord Provost, thanked the deputation for attending the meeting, and for the assurance they had given. He said it was at times like these in Britain's history that we really appreciated what it meant to have a united body of citizens.

TENEMENT PROTECTION

The Executive Committee considered many other matters, important among which was the question of permanent shelters for backgreens. The design of a permanent type was submitted, and the opinion of the Home Office, under whose direction these shelters are erected, is to be asked.

This form of shelter, it is estimated, will hold 50 persons each, and in the view of those responsible for its design will form a useful adjunct to shelters already being erected by the Town Council. These sandbag barricades are, however, an obstacle to pedestrian traffic on pavements, and the new shelter, which would be in the back green, is considered to be an admirable substitute, and to be equally, if not more, efficient. Meantime the City Engineer, under the direction of Councillors James Miller and Johnston Gilbert, is continuing to provide protection for citizens in the shortest possible time.

ALL SERVICES READY

It was stated rescue and repair squads were standing by as requested by the Government, and were in a position to tackle any reasonable call on their services. The fire service was reported to be functioning well, the whole personnel being called up. A considerable amount of work had to be done in billeting the men, but this had been successfully carried out. Wardens' posts were manned and a 24 hours' service was in operation in all divisions of the city.

The Executive had been developing a scheme for aiding any families in distress as the result of air raid damage. Five centres—schools and church halls—will be instituted as clearing houses, and those rendered homeless will be sent there and will be looked after until alternative accommodation — either by billeting or transfer to another house— is found.

It was reported that 470,000 respirators had been issued. This number did not include children under five, supplies for whom are not yet available.

LIGHTING RESTRICTIONS

In an interview the Chief Air Raid Warden expressed himself as very well satisfied with the response of the various services to the recent call. He urged all members to read the A.R.P. Guide, particularly the portions which refer to their service, and make themselves acquainted with the details of the scheme.

"It cannot be over-emphasised," said Mr Falconer, "that we are now operating under war conditions, and, under these conditions, all orders must be instantly obeyed. This applies particularly to the lighting restrictions. This is not a matter in which preparations may now be made. If the preparations have not been fully made, other drastic alternatives must be applied. Removal of all electric bulbs will ensure that lights will not be used until the necessary steps for darkening windows, etc., have been taken. All stair lights must be kept extinguished, and cupolas completely shut off where lights in halls, etc., are still to be used.

"The lighting restrictions imposed in connection with motor vehicles are now being rigidly enforced, and drivers who have not already taken the necessary precautions will be precluded from using their cars at all after sunset.

"There is no doubt," he concluded, "that the public will support the authorities in every endeavour they are making for the safety of citizens. This is no time for delay."

NO ONE O'CLOCK GUN

From now until further notice the one o'clock time gun at Edinburgh Castle will not be fired. The Public Relations Officer of the Scottish Command Headquarters issued this statement to-day.

PREMIER AND HITLERISM

In a speech to the House of Commons the Prime Minister dramatically confirmed that the country was at war, and said: "I trust I may see the day when Hitlerism is destroyed. The Government would without hesitation fulfil their obligations to Poland. As I said the other day, we are ready. This is a sad day for all of us.

ESSENTIAL MATERIALS

SUPPLY MINISTER APPOINTS CONTROLLERS

The Ministry of Supply has made orders for the control of essential materials, including iron and steel, wool, jute, silk, rayon, timber, paper, and leather. Controllers have been appointed for the various materials.

Other articles covered by the orders are non-ferrous metals (copper, lead, and zinc), aluminium, flax, hemp, molasses, and industrial alcohol.

The main objects of the control are the regulation of prices and distribution of supplies equitably throughout the trades.

Paris police are all equipped with steel helmets and carry their gas masks.

NEW ZEALAND'S SUPPORT

The ordinary and special reservists of the New Zealand regular forces have been called up.

The acting Prime Minister, Mr P. Fraser, stated in Auckland that New Zealand had informed Britain of her entire approval of the course taken by the British Government, and had promised the fullest support of the Dominion.

The Most Rev. Dr Averill, Primate of New Zealand, has urged that special services be held in all churches to-morrow, and that all Christians be called upon to make an intensified intercession for peace.

No one sentenced in connection with I.R.A. outrages is among those to be discharged.

SIGNOR GAYDA'S VIEW

"ONLY MIRACLE CAN AVOID GENERAL EXPLOSION"

Signor Gayda (Mussolini's mouthpiece), writing in this morning's "Giornale d'Italia," said:

"The Franco-British ultimatum to Berlin foreshadows the development of the conflict to such an extent that only a miracle can avoid a general explosion.

"For five months Germany left the door open for negotiations, consultations, discussions, and decisions. For the same period Italy has been doing her utmost by diplomatic action in Warsaw, warning of the seriousness of the situation, and advising the Polish Government to start negotiations."

PUBLIC WARNED

NON-OBSERVANCE OF BLACK-OUT RULES

STRICT ENFORCEMENT, AND PENALTIES

A notice issued by the Lord Privy Seal's Department to-day states that reports from many Air Raid Precautions authorities indicate that black-out regulations are not being properly observed by members of the public.

The following are some typical cases of imperfect obscuration:

Shaded lights behind yellow blinds.

Bars of light showing above dark curtains.

Motorists who switch on lights inside their garages while putting their cars away.

Snack bars and similar premises open to the street which dim the light in the bar itself but allow a bright light to shine out from the back rooms, etc.

Front doors of houses and shops opened, allowing light to stream out from the inside.

PRISON AND £100 FINES

It also appears, the notice says, that some persons whose attention was called to imperfect screening of lights did not recognise that it was now the law that required the lights to be obscured and that there were penalties for breach of the law.

Failure to comply with the regulations involves, on summary conviction, liability to imprisonment for a term not exceeding three months, or a fine not exceeding £100, or both. On conviction on indictment, anyone guilty of an offence against the regulations is liable to imprisonment for a term not exceeding two years, or to a fine not exceeding £500, or both.

Moreover, if the lighting order made under Defence Regulation 24 is not complied with in the case of any premises, vehicle, or vessel, any constable and any member of his Majesty's forces may enter the premises or board the vehicle or vessel and take all steps as may be reasonably necessary for the enforcement of the lighting order.

Motorists are once again advised that if they wish to use their cars they must take the steps to obscure the lighting of their vehicles. In accordance with the regulations, it will be strongly enforced from sunset to-night.

—*WHY*

do advertisers and readers agree that the Edinburgh Evening News is the finest value in evening newspapers to be had in Edinburgh and district

✥   ✥   ✥

READERS *choose*

. . . . the *Edinburgh Evening News* because it gives the best coverage of all local and national events, and because they have known for years that it is a newspaper on which they can rely. Readers also know that they can save money by studying the advertising columns of the *News* regularly, because they find there the widest selection of all those things they need to buy or sell, from property to pins. No wonder they choose the . . . .

ADVERTISERS *use*

. . . . the *Edinburgh Evening News* because it is the most widely read evening paper in the district and therefore has the greatest pulling power.

Wise business men realise that in these days of intense competition it is not enough to keep old customers, but they must also attract new ones, by advertising. There is no easier, cheaper way of getting new customers in Edinburgh and district than by regular advertising in the . . . .

Edinburgh Evening News

The Evening Newspaper with the greatest pulling power in Edinburgh and Eastern Scotland

PALESTINE ARABS

OFFERS OF HELP TO THE BRITISH

A telegram from the High Commissioner for Palestine reports that Abdul Raouf Effendi Bitar, chairman of the Jaffa Municipal Commission, and other notables, called on Mr C. B. Norman, Acting District Commissioner Lydda District, and requested that a body of voluntary civil workers should be enrolled at Jaffa to be available as A.R.P. workers and for other duties. As a result the registration of volunteers began at the district office to-day.

About 150 notables of Nablus and the surrounding district met in the Municipal Office at Nablus and appointed a deputation under the Mayor, Suliman Bey Tukan, to meet the Acting District Commissioner, who was asked to convey to the Government the readiness of the majority of Arabs in the Samaria district to place their services at the disposal of Great Britain in the event of war.

Nuri Pasha, the Iraqi Premier, announced in Baghdad that Iraq would give Britain all available help inside Iraq.

MORE INDIAN PRINCES SUPPORT BRITAIN

Assurances of loyalty and offers of support for the King-Emperor have been received from 18 more Indian Princes. They include the Maharajah Jam Saheb of Nawanagar and the Maharajah of Jaipur.

At least 46 Indian rulers have now offered their services to Britain.—Reuter.

ULSTER SOLID

The Northern Ireland Parliament will meet on Monday to pass emergency legislation for Northern Ireland for defence purposes in support of Great Britain.

No question of neutrality arises. The Government is solidly behind Mr Chamberlain, and is in close touch with the Imperial Government.

Printed and published at 18 Market Street, Edinburgh, for the proprietors, Provincial Newspapers Limited, 2 Salisbury Square, London, E.C.4.

Reproduced on the occasion of the 100th birthday of the Edinburgh Evening News, May 27th 1973.

The start of hostilities did not darken the skies with German bombers as was expected, but only a matter of hours after Chamberlain's sombre Sunday morning declaration it was harshly confirmed to Scotland that the worst could happen at any time. Distress signals picked up from the Atlantic confirmed to the Naval authorities that the liner *Athenia*, Canada-bound from Liverpool, had been torpedoed with heavy loss of life.

The shock of the survivors being unloaded at Greenock, the lack of preparation to receive them, and their vivid accounts of the U-boat attack made an enormous impact. People had looked to the skies for danger, but it had come sinisterly from the depths and struck indiscriminately and without warning. At first the reaction was outrage, then cold anger. Suddenly the war was real and close and personal. Yet if the Germans thought perhaps it would sap morale it had the opposite effect. There could have been no greater spur to the country to throw itself into war preparations than what was seen as a cowardly attack against a defenceless ship.

> "I was only a boy when war was declared and it was all a bit confusing. I knew my parents were very concerned but it did not seem to make much difference to my life. Then I heard a ship called the *Athenia* had been sunk by a U-boat. I had always been scared of water and I remember thinking how terrible. After that, although I was only ten, I wanted to punch Hitler on the nose."
>
> *Glasgow Postal Worker*

EDINBURGH EVENING NEWS. MONDAY, SEPTEMBER 4, 1939   PAGE 5

GLASGOW LINER FIRST U-BOAT VICTIM

Parliament's Indignation at Athenia Outrage

NO WARNING GIVEN

Mr Churchill and "Inhumane" Circumstances

NOT AN ARMED MERCHANTMAN

Earl Stanhope and Another Broken Pledge

A 13,000-TONNER

MINISTERS CARRY GAS MASKS

WASHINGTON TOLD

EARLY WORKING OF CONVOY SYSTEM

LETITIA TURNED BACK

RUTHLESS WARFARE

SINKING OF LUSITANIA RECALLED

24. The torpedoed *Athenia* sinks by the stern 200 miles west of the Hebrides.

ARP and the Home Guard

> "We had to build our own air-raid shelter and when we saw the bit of corrugated iron and the pieces of wood we felt we would be just as safe inside the house. Then we heard that blast was the big danger from bombs and that it turned houses to matchsticks. After that my husband got busy with his spade, but to me the shelter looked too much like a grave for comfort."
>
> *Former Glasgow Munitions Worker*

> "I was eight years of age when war broke out. My brother and I had the job of filling sandbags at the weekend for our own house and for some of the neighbours. We took them round in my home-made bogey. I don't know if you have ever tried to lift a sandbag, but they were very heavy and it was really hard work. No wonder a sandbag wall was such a good defence against bullets and shrapnel."
>
> *Dundee Resident*

25. Edinburgh's combined civil defence forces are inspected by Prime Minister Winston Churchill on the Castle Esplanade, 12 October 1942.

"I remember as a boy fitting on my new gas mask. My recollection is that it was horrible. It smelt of rubber and we had to keep it on for a while to get used to it. When no one was looking I used to lift a corner and suck in fresh air. What a relief! Someone said that the bottom of the mask could turn poisonous if it was not changed at regular intervals and that worried me more than the thought of a gas attack. It did not take my friends long to discover that the rubber sides could make loud rude noises when breathing out, which was good for a snigger and took our minds off the seriousness of it all."

Dundee Hospital Worker

Civil Defence
Inspection by
Prime Minister

Chamberlain's brittle voice announcing that once more we were reluctantly at war with Germany meant much had to be done quickly to put the country on a full operational war footing. Having witnessed the brutality that befell those countries which tried to impede Hitler's aspirations it was fully expected that the first air-raids would commence within hours and that gas attacks would follow soon afterwards. Death-from-the-skies warfare, it was estimated, would cause nearly 250,000 casualties in the first week of bombing.

Hopes lingered to the last that somehow war could be averted, but the attack on the Poles conditioned people to anticipate the worst and the urgent need to make ready for unknown battlefronts in Europe as well as on the home front was only too obvious. The country, therefore, threw itself into preparations.

From the mid Thirties the possibility of a second great war had looked increasingly likely and by that fateful 1938 Munich summit steps were already being taken in Scotland to substantially increase aircraft production, shipbuilding and munitions manufacture.

By August 1939 this was all developing into a frenzy of activity as the crisis mounted. Reservists were called up, the ARP (Air-Raid Precautions) wardens were placed on stand-by and plans put into gear for the issue of gas masks, identity cards, the building of air-raid shelters, creating a night time 'blackout' and for the evacuation of children from cities.

Twelve evacuation camps in Scotland were scheduled for the end of the year and twenty new hospitals with 7,000 beds were to be ready 'just in case', with a further accommodation of 10,000 beds in huts for completion shortly afterwards. Before hostilities commenced, around 10,000 trained nurses had enrolled and 45,000 auxiliaries were ready to train.

Back in July the call had gone out for volunteers for all forms of National Service and by the beginning of 1 August 380,000 people had stepped forward and were signing up at the rate of 20,000 a week. Now two highly-motivated and efficient armies were required: the first to tackle the Germans head on at the frontline with bomb and tank and bullet, the other to keep them there by providing the support, the guns, the ammunition and that essential will to win.

The scale of this citizens' war and the degree of help required was quickly appreciated: in peacetime the Scottish fire brigade strength was about 21,000, but the war-footing estimate of auxiliary services needed was 300,000; peacetime police strength was some 70,000 officers and at least a further auxiliary 200,000 were now demanded. In the Home Front war the politicians had no cause for concern over the public's sense of duty. In the aftermath of recession they had precious little to thank the politicians for, but where the country's security was involved their support came in a flood.

On 24 August Parliament passed the Emergency Powers (Defence) Act which gave it wide-sweeping rights to take virtually any step it deemed necessary in defence of the realm and the security of its citizens. Within days a flurry of regulations demonstrated that it had every intention of doing just that.

Restriction and detention orders often caused anguish and the issue generated fierce political debate. In the end, Lord Shaw of Dunfermline probably analysed the dilemma as concisely as anyone: "Here is a situation where the Executive becomes both gaoler and judge", he said. "It must be recognised that where the safety of the State is concerned it may be necessary to act upon suspicion instead of upon complete proof. Defence may be more important than liberty."

With the stormtroopers straining at the leash, the fearful examples of what had happened to the Jews and the Czechs and the Führer's obvious determination to commit his

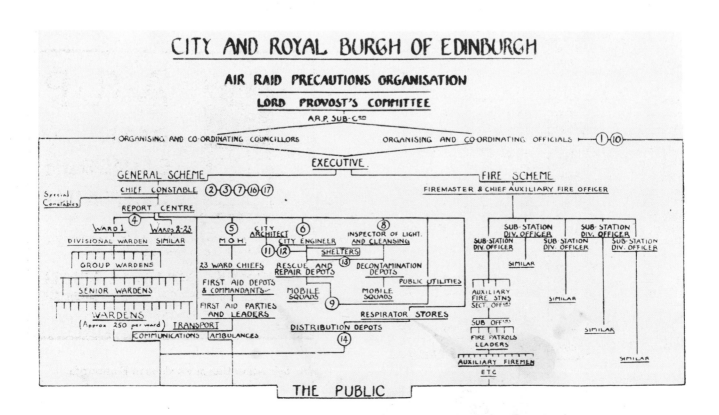

VII. APPROXIMATE ALLOCATION OF WARDENS

No.	Wards.	Population.	Acreage.	Reqd. Men & Women.	No. of Groups.	Posts & Sectors.
1.	Calton	20,000	228	240	6	40
2.	Canongate	18,000	965	216	5	36
3.	Newington	23,000	891	276	8	46
4.	Morningside	26,000	1,358	312	8	52
5.	Merchiston	24,000	677	288	8	48
6.	Gorgie	28,000	676	336	6	56
7.	Haymarket	23,000	959	276	7	40
8.	St. Bernard's	22,000	1,250	264	5	44
9.	Broughton	18,000	472	216	7	36
10.	St. Stephen's	17,000	190	204	6	34
11.	St. Andrew's	14,000	206	168	5	29
12.	St. Giles'	17,000	266	204	4	34
13.	Dalry	19,000	187	228	4	38
14.	George Square	19,000	248	228	3	38
15.	St. Leonard's	16,000	104	192	4	32
16.	Portobello	34,000	2,200	408	6	68
17.	South Leith	28,000	819	336	4	56
18.	North Leith	15,000	218	180	3	30
19.	West Leith	18,000	462	216	6	36
20.	Central Leith	12,000	142	144	4	24
21.	Liberton	17,000	6,339	204	10	34
22.	Colinton	12,000	5,602	144	5	26
23.	Corstorphine and Cramond	30,000	8,067	360	11	60
	TOTALS	470,000	32,526	5,740	135	937

Wardens, Men		4,592
Women		1,148
Reserves		1,435
	TOTAL	7,175

27. *above:* Fire tender number 3 of the City of Dunfermline Fire Brigade, with Firemaster Muir on the pump trailer.

28. *left:* Allocation of wardens in Edinburgh.

30, 31 & 32. *top, middle and bottom:* "The Cads" of No 2 Patrol, "The Calamity Squad" of No 3 Patrol and "The Awkward Squad" of No 4 Patrol, Edinburgh Fire Brigade and Auxiliary Fire Service, at the outbreak of war in 1939. Spirits were high and they were ready for the worst the Germans might offer.

33. *opposite page, top:* Prime Minister Winston Churchill inspects civil defence units in Edinburgh,1943. He is accompanied by Chief Constable W B R Morren and Lord Provost Sir Will Y Darling dressed in military uniform as Lord Lieutenant.

34. *opposite page, bottom:* Visit by H M King George VI and Queen Elizabeth to inspect civil defence units in Edinburgh.

35. Where firefighting was concerned, any equipment that was handy and could do the job was requisitioned. This American Packard automobile had power, speed and a roof strong enough to carry a ladder. Leading Fireman Jack Watson, of Edinburgh, is ready to take it into action with its crew.

36. Winners . . . a section of firewomen of the National Fire Service were all smiles in Edinburgh after winning a fire pump competition in 1944. Women took their places as firefighters beside men if necessary, although most undertook various other duties like driving, stores and canteen service.

37. Cuppa time at the mobile kitchen for members of the South Eastern area of the Scottish National Fire Service. This particular canteen unit as gifted by the citizens of Guelph and Wellington County in Ontario, Canada. The picture is taken in the yard at Lauriston Fire Station, Edinburgh. 38. *below:* Nursing auxiliaries inspected by Churchill, Edinburgh, 1943.

39. *right:* All hands to the pipes . . . in case service was impeded by the fracture of water mains during enemy action, an emergency water supply was devised for major cities. These water pipes could be laid in the gutters for ready access. This picture was taken in Edinburgh — which held a record for pipe-laying.

40. *below:* Photographed in Edinburgh, a Gorgie-based unit of the Auxiliary Fire Service on parade with their borrowed lorry, roped-in portable fire pump and some coils of canvas hose of dubious quality; note the white-walled tyres and mudguards to make the vehicle visible in blackout conditions.

armies to achieve his vision of German supremacy in Europe, the outrage which Lord Shaw's statement would have caused in peace time was tempered by grudging recognition of the reality of confrontation with a megalomaniac who knew no rules, had no scruples, no sense of morality and no scale of proportion.

The Royal Navy steamed up the Forth to put on a show of muscle-power with visits from the *Ark Royal* (our newest aircraft carrier), cruisers *Aurora, Boreas, Samali, Glasgow, Jervis, Bandit* and *Jackal* and the second submarine flotilla. When the old HMS *Edinburgh* arrived, tour parties left the Hawes Pier at South Queensferry to clamber over the great warrior and wonder at its might. The resultant press publicity snarled that Hitler would certainly not have it all his own way.

When it was flashed to the Royal Navy that Chamberlain had at last — with a push — assembled his War Cabinet and that Winston Churchill, out of office for a decade because of his warlike tones and imperialistic views, had returned to his old World War One job as First Lord of the Admiralty, a thrill of expectancy passed through all ranks. "Winston is back!" said the signal and its effect was immediate. As one sailor put it: "We had always been confident. Suddenly we were cocky."

The War Budget was raising income tax at its highest ever level of 7s 6d in the pound; the IRA was having a deadly bombing campaign on mainland Britain; Glenn Miller recorded *In the Mood*; the first aeroplane powered by jet engine took to the skies — the German Heinkel He-187; in Spain, General Franco executed 53 people for the murder of a police chief. And on the Home Front a great digging of air-raid shelters and filling of sandbags was taking place. There was a dedicated reading of government literature on air-raid warnings, gas masks, lighting restriction, fire precautions and first aid. A vast training for auxiliaries in every branch was programmed. Road blocks and seaside defences were being constructed; and a welter of information by government pamphlets, radio and newspapers bombarded the public advising on almost every aspect of the conduct of war from dealing with spies to improving eyesight in the blackouts by eating carrots. And all the time the people of Britain waited for the first eerie wail of the siren.

In Edinburgh public air-raid shelters were provided for 30,000 people and private shelters for 110,000. Even Princes Street Gardens were dug up, along with back greens and lawns throughout the city. There were many complaints in the early days about the ARP, including payment, but the chief warden hit back and told the Capital's citizens that they should have more regard for the services. "We owe them our deepest gratitude" he said. "We should not forget that 85 per cent of the wardens service, 80 per cent of the first aid service and 50 per cent of the fire service is purely voluntary and unpaid. This should be remembered by those who are willing to offer criticism but not service, particularly voluntary service." Millions of people throughout the country slept more peacefully at night, it was pointed out, because they knew that these public-spirited guards were patrolling the streets and standing by at wardens' first aid and fire-fighting posts.

During that summer of blue skies and high temperatures

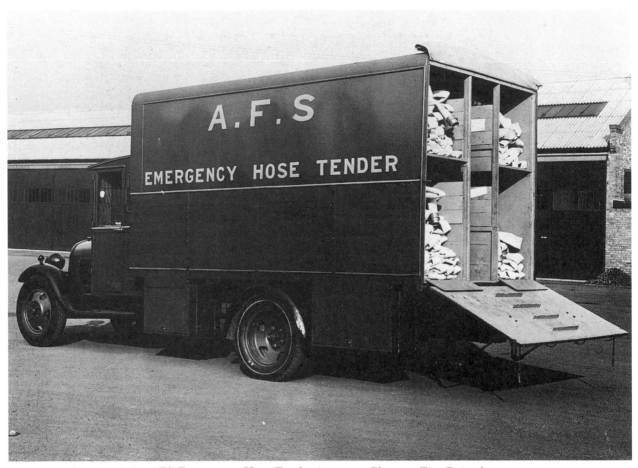

43 AFS Emergency Hose Tender in use at Glasgow Fire Brigade.

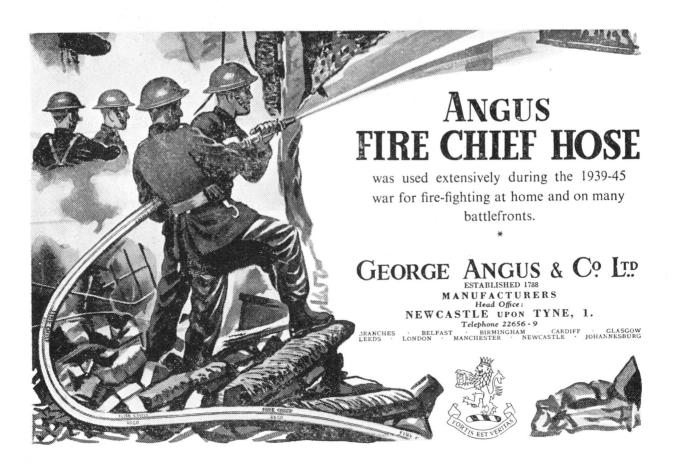

45. A jolly Christmas card for 1943 showing that all was not just doom and gloom.

it was the great emptying of the children from our cities in an evacuation programme which made the most marked impact on the public. The 1,400 civilians who had died in the 103 air-raids by the 'toy' planes of the First World War had created the unnerving and lasting impression that comprehensive bombing of populated areas was certain to be used as a standard weapon in future.

Since 1924 plans had been laid for the evacuation of children from the main target zones, and improvements in warplanes meant the threat was very real. In January and February 1939 the call went out for volunteers to take evacuees and compulsory billeting became a possibility under Section 56 of the Civil Defence Act, with the threat of £50 fines or a three-month jail sentence for not adhering to the terms.

The evacuation of thousands of children from the cities, dramatically plucked from their families, set down among strangers in strange surroundings in far-distant locations with little communication, was a social earthquake. It was heart-rending for both parents and children, and it was acceptable only because the heartache, the worry, the difficulties and fears were preferable to the prospect of the children becoming part of the target for German bombs.

The nation had never witnessed such scenes: long crocodiles of packaged children, neatly labelled, gas masks over shoulders, the younger ones bewildered, clinging to favourite toys and bags of goodies, some in tears. The older ones, who understood the reason and need to be torn from their homes, tried to disguise their emotions with difficulty, while some stout hearts were caught up in the general excitement, enjoying it all immensely. Fretting mothers held back tears, as serious-faced fathers wondered if they would see their offspring again before they, too, were spirited off to some distant frontline. There were fussing teachers checking lists, names, baggage and destinations; helpful, controlled policemen, supervisors and railway staff solving the practical difficulties, getting the trains moving.

The plan for evacuation, which was not compulsory, divided Scotland into three sections — sending, neutral and receiving areas. Five areas were to be evacuated: Glasgow, Edinburgh, Dundee, Clydebank and Rosyth.

Glasgow, which had a tenement population alone of 600,000, had by far the largest number of 'vaccies' who were destined for far-flung receiving areas stretching from Wigtown to the Buchan coast, some heading to Perthshire, Argyll and Dumfries, others to Bute and Deeside. The estimate was that it would take three days to clear them all. Edinburgh's evacuees were sent to the Lothians, Peebles, Selkirk, Roxburgh, Berwick and Fife. The authorities reckoned evacuation could be completed in two days. Dundee

Seasons Greetings

South Eastern Fire Force SCOTLAND

NFS

CHRISTMAS 1943

WOODCROFT, CLINTON ROAD, EDINBURGH

was the smallest area and the aim there was to take two days to uplift their children to the receiving areas of Angus and Kincardine.

Over in Glasgow, on 1 September, the plan was for the first groups of children to muster at their schools by 6.30 am. Seventy thousand children from the 'bull's eye' area close to the Clyde were to be loaded into 102 special trains. Suddenly there was a blanket shortage and children over twelve were asked to take one with them in addition to spare clothes and something to eat on the journey. As war appeared an increasing certainty more and more Glaswegians, who had regarded the whole exercise as a waste of time, began to have second thoughts. An unexpected 23,000 late-comers met with the cheery response that all were welcome.

Lord Provost Pat Dollan assured parents that everything possible was being done for the children's safety and comfort. "My wife has gone round towns in the south of Scotland" he told them, "and she has just telephoned me to say that parents need have no anxiety regarding the manner in which children will be cared for. Everything has been prepared down to the last detail."

He was right. The operation went like clockwork. The organisation was remarkable. The first contingent was to arrive at Stirling at 10.58 am, where clerks in the public assistance department of Stirling county council slept overnight in their offices at Viewforth to be ready for the onslaught. By 4.00 pm six more trainloads had arrived.

The plan was for the first consignment of the 30,000 children and 10,000 mothers sent to Aberdeen to arrive at 3.00 pm to meet fourteen trains that would convey them up-line to Aboyne for dispersal. Around 2,000 more were to detrain in Cults, Culter and Torphins. Rothesay accepted some 5,000, Campbeltown and Kintyre 1,500, while a reception centre at Ayr ice rink purveyed tea, coffee, milk and emergency rations to their 3,168.

In Edinburgh the abrupt marshalling instructions for the first wave of schools was as follows:-

"The undernoted are the times and railway stations for the departure of school children under the evacuation scheme, 7.00 am assembly:

All Saints School — Princess Street; Canonmills School — Waverley; Castlehill — Waverley; Corstorphine — Corstorphine; Craigentinny — Piershill; Gorgie — Gorgie; Hermitage Park — Leith Central; Longstone — Gorgie LNER; Niddrie — Duddingston; North Merchiston — Merchiston; Parsons Green — Piershill; Roseburn — Murrayfield; South Bridge — Waverley."

There are many stations on that list which no longer exist in the Edinburgh of today, but for the children who took part in that great exodus to safety from all our cities the details remain vivid: the banging of gas masks against their sides; the pictures of Scottish holiday scenes on the station

47. At the beginning of the war gas masks were an essential feature of air-raid precautions but during the course of the war fears of gas attacks diminished and they were regarded as more of a nuisance and an encumbrance.

billboards and in the train carriages; the excruciating restraint required not to eat the 'picnic' emergency rations before the train had even left the station; the quiet orderliness of the whole operation; the worry that identity labels might be lost and young lives spent aimlessly on trains for ever; the worried look on parents' faces; shouts of "this way for the pleasure trip special"; children crying, laughing, thumb-sucking furiously; whistles blowing, white handkerchiefs waving, the concerns as well as the anticipation of the unknown; in short, the enormous adventure of it all.

In Midlothian, Lady Elphinstone, the county organiser for women's voluntary services, waiting to receive her small army, sent out an SOS for volunteers who could cook, do laundry work, mend and were talented at amusing children. "We're short of 4,000 mattresses and 12,000 blankets", she said, and then with an admonition: "Tell those Edinburgh women to hurry up and send us blankets. It's their children we are going to take care of. We're doing the work, surely they can provide the bedding."

Walter Elliot, Minister of State at the time, had a message for everyone: "Don't use the telephone or telegraph more than you can help. Whatever happens the work of the country must go on. The motto is stand by your posts. By Monday night we will have given the world another example of what a free people can do that puts its back into the work and its heart into the job."

As an example of detailed exit planning, it was a model of efficiency. However, all did not go quite so smoothly at the receiving end: there were reports of Roman Catholic families being sent into Protestant areas, resulting in a different kind of battlefront; children from slum areas being sent to large villas where they conversed in awed whispers for weeks; complaints that some teachers regarded it all as a holiday and, like some of the evacuated mothers, appeared to absolve themselves of responsibility for their charges.

There were scattered tales of extreme loneliness, homesickness, incompatibility and, sometimes, harsh treatment.

It was not long before the discovery was made that something dreadful was amiss. The first clues came on examination of the list of items the children were advised to take with them: "A warm coat or mackintosh, a change of underclothes and stockings, handkerchieves, night clothes, house shoes or rubber shoes, toothbrush, comb, towel, soap, face cloth and a tin cup." What was being revealed from all the sending areas, but with particular reference to Glasgow, was that many of the children did not have warm coats, far less night clothes and slippers. Some stepped out of the trains in the only clothes they possessed and they were verminous and dirty. Many of the children had head-lice, others fleas and body-lice, some had contagious diseases and a few were so ill they should have been in sanitoriums.

For the first time the scandal of the conditions in Scotland's cities was being put on full public display and the rest of the country was shocked. A report from a Stirling Town Council meeting summed it up: "It has lifted the veil on the lives of thousands of the populace, disclosing such conditions of squalor, disease, dirt and ignorance of the elementary laws of health and decent living that it has appalled those of us who have had to cope with it . . . we would all willingly have become evacuees ourselves to escape from the hundreds of frantic householders asking what we were going to do about ridding them of the lice and filth that had invaded their homes." Even for seasoned nurses the de-lousing process of parents, children and bedding was too much. Some receiving householders asked for children to be removed, others rolled up their sleeves and got busy with soap, hot water, paraffin and steel combs. Some children had the humiliation of having their heads shaved and received permission to go to school wearing a

48. An Anderson shelter, and its occupier, in an Edinburgh garden.

"I'VE ALWAYS WANTED TO SEE INTO THIS HOUSE!"

"Happy at your work, Mac?"

burgh Evening

TUESDAY, SEPTEMBER 5, 1939

POINTS

ard but for omit-
en Championship,
most successful
ar in 1936. Then
g worth winning,
prize of all—the
t he was out of
time, his loss of
o staleness after
a. However, the
ck to form with a
off by winning
000 Tournament
d Burton. His
Brighton, is still
included a second
d Padgham his
team.

nounced yester-

LAST WARNING TO CITIZENS

"Black-Out" Most Unsatisfactory

Following a detailed observation by the Royal Air Force on the effectiveness of the black-out as applied to Edinburgh, it has been reported to the Chief Constable that the result is "most unsatisfactory." The report states that, generally speaking, lights were visible throughout the whole city, and vehicles in particular were clearly visible.

The R.A.F. go on to state that as a result of their observations they were clearly over a city. This state of affairs is most reprehensible, and reveals a com-

9, 50. *top left and above:* Humorous observations of
he time.

1. *top right:* Initially, the blackout in Edinburgh
as unsatisfactory.

2. *right:* A notice printed in the *Evening Dispatch*.

CITY OF EDINBURGH

AIR RAID PRECAUTIONS

BLACK-OUT

In order to assist in obtaining Black-Out conditions in the City, it would be an advantage if BACKGREEN DOORS which are usually kept locked at night, could be left OPEN so that Police and Wardens can have access to the backs of the Tenements and ensure that windows are properly screened.

It is in the interest of every Citizen that proper Safety Precautions should be taken.

W. B. R. MORREN, Chief Constable.

53. Fire at Jeffreys Brewery in Edinburgh, October 1941.

cap or headscarf in class. Some were tormented by local children. Some adapted quickly, became close members of their temporarily adopted families, and retained friendships. Some remained to the end of the war, enjoying it all, and they still visit old friends.

The authorities argued public duty in response to most of the complaints. "Do your best", they said, "and remember that to return the evacuees to their homes will endanger their lives from enemy bombs. The cities could turn into rubble at any moment. Liken the situation to the soldier in the front line. He is given a wet, dirty, verminous trench to hold. Is he going to say —I am returning to base unless you give me a warm, dry trench?" It was a form of blackmail, of course, but in wartime there was little else the authorities or the people could do but make the best of a bad situation — especially when the reports from Europe demonstrated daily that millions were in much worse situations.

Nonetheless, the insight that the rest of Scotland had into the lives and living conditions of thousands of people in our cities was a revelation. It was repugnant, degrading and

unacceptable. In a country which thought its social reforms were in advance of most others, the realisation of the awful truth was both a shock and an embarrassment. Other countries were taking positive and pioneering strides forward. We had still to develop a proper health education programme. Even now, with the perspective of fifty years, the affront of those reprehensible conditions, the lack of basic health and hygiene knowledge exposed by the evacuations still remains a disgrace.

As it turned out, the cities were not immediately bombed and as the 'Phoney War' dragged on families began to question the need and pain of the separation, and a trickle made their way home, although by January 1940 only ten per cent of Glasgow's evacuees had returned.

In July 1939 the first 2,860 young men aged between twenty and twenty-one from cities and towns all over Scotland commenced their six months' training as militiamen. There were the appropriate scenes of enthusiasm at Glencorse, Hamilton, Perth, Ayr, Berwick, Aberdeen, Maryhill, Stirling, Inverness and Fort George. Even the

54. Firefighting train demonstration, October 1941.

Records and Pay Office at Leith Fort took ten. This was effectively the start of the build-up to full-scale conscription but, unlike 1917, only a limited number of volunteers were accepted at first.

Two months later upon the outbreak of war, Parliament passed the National Service (Armed Forces) Act under which all men aged between eighteen and forty-one were liable for call-up. The *Stirling Journal* reported on 7 September 1939 that two thirds of those who tried to enlist at Stirling were turned away, although regulars or skilled tradesmen of all kinds, including drivers, could be accepted for the duration of the war. Those rejected were given a free ticket home. Wisely, time was being taken to blunt initial eagerness and assess what requirements were also needed on the Home Front. By the end of the year, however, over one and a half million men were receiving a taste of service discipline.

The registration of all men in each age group in turn began on 21 October, when those between twenty and twenty-three were called up if they were fit enough. It was June 1941 before forty-year-olds were reached. There was some early concern that those who enlisted for Scottish regiments were being sent to England because of lack of

57. *above:* Emerging from the shelters, Princess Street Gardens, Edinburgh.

56. *opposite page:* Sandbags and air-raid shelters in an Edinburgh back court. There had been extensive building of air-raid shelters even before war was declared. These brick shelters were less flimsy than the Anderson shelters but would not withstand a direct hit.

accommodation, and wrangles about exemption continued until the end of the war. The full authority of the law was invoked to solve some troublesome situations, but the onus was always on the individual to do his duty. In one case before the Appellate Tribunal for conscientious objectors in Edinburgh's Parliament House, a Jehovah's Witness shipping clerk pleaded that his sole purpose in life was to serve God, which to him was the most important thing in his existence.

"You would not be prevented from preaching the gospel if you joined the army", said the judge.

"I don't think I could accept military service with my views" replied the clerk. "The only way I can preach the gospel is by going from door to door."

"You could go from man to man", decided the judge and dismissed the appeal. It also has to be said that many conscientious objectors who could not bring themselves to take up arms nonetheless gave distinguished war service as stretcher bearers and members of the Pioneer Corps. Some, of course, preferred prison.

To release fighting troops it made sense to utilise as many of the 'old brigade' as possible in civil defence roles, and as early as October 1939 Churchill had a 'Dad's Army' in mind. When the LDVs (Local Defence Volunteers) were formed in May 1940 there was an immediate rush of recruits, many of them army veterans, who had much to offer, although they were not so young as they used to be. The upper age limit was supposedly sixty-five, but the rule was interpreted loosely, and one old-timer sergeant major from Crieff had even been in the Egyptian campaign of 1884. Churchill, in a speech in July, referred to them as the 'Home Guard' and the name stuck.

Captain Mainwaring of television's *Dad's Army* fame and his platoon of all-sorts held them up to affectionate ridicule, but in effect it was a larger-than-life version of the real thing. At the outset they were short of equipment, the unit leadership was suspect, discipline was patchy, at times they sported an unusual array of weaponry and they did find themselves in amusing situations. There was a deadly serious side, however, and they were also quite clear that if enemy paratroopers or an invasion force landed they would be in the thick of the action. Armies are blunt instruments and they destroy if they can whatever is in their way, irrespective of age or background. Apart from the valuable guarding and lookout duties the Home Guard were also resigned to fight or be killed. By the middle of the war they were a much improved and valuable force.

58. Dunbartonshire Local Defence Volunteers, June 1940.

59. A devastating show of strength by the Home Guard unit at John Lewis shipbuilders in Aberdeen.

60. Local Defence Volunteer Walter Rankin, painted by Sir W O Hutchison, 1940. This picture most successfully captured the spirit of "Dad's Army" and hangs in the Scottish National Portrait Gallery.

61. Local Defence Volunteers' first practise shoot at Hunter's Bog. Officers and other ranks from the Greenend area of Edinburgh are pictured practising with borrowed rifles. This group of LDVs eventually became 'G' Coy, 6th Btn Home Guard.

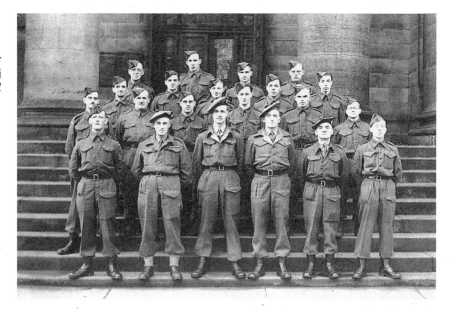

62. 'A' Coy, 6th Btn Home Guard. *front row, left to right:* Sgt Jim Clark, Maj Ian Fraser, Lieut John Stewart, Maj Bill Benzies, Lieut John Rhind, Sgt Don Stewart. *second row, third from left:* Ron Turnbull.

63. Local Defence Volunteers man the observation post at Edinburgh's Dean Bridge.

64. ARP Wardens at Andrew Wilson, caterers, outside their Edinburgh Spring Garden premises.

65. An invitation to combine the need for carrying a gas mask with sartorial elegance.

"When war was declared I overheard my father telling my mother that once food rationing started all the pets would have to be destroyed. I was horrified. At the time I had a dog and a budgie and my first thought was to run away with them. Thank goodness it never happened. Our old dog Sandy died of old age a couple of months later. The Lord Provost of Perth used to get millet for his budgie out of the same wee shop in South Street where I went."
Perth Resident

CAN A WARDEN BE A GOOD WIFE?

Mrs. X discovers how !

The Bombing

The shooting war came to Scotland dramatically on 16 October 1939. That morning Flight Lieutenant G C Pinkerton was patrolling around 9.45 am off the Isle of May in a Spitfire of 602 (City of Glasgow) Squadron from RAF Drem, near North Berwick, when out of the North Sea mists he was suddenly confronted by an enemy plane. With a loud 'tallyho' signal to ground control he engaged the plane with gusto. The German veered to port and escaped into cloud, smoke trailing, leaving Flight Lieutenant Pinkerton extremely disappointed at missing the first 'kill' of the war.

The disappointment did not last long. That afternoon the Germans were back in greater force in their first raid on Britain — a mixture of Heinkel IIIs, Dornier 215s and Junker 88s heading for the Forth Bridge, Rosyth and HMS *Edinburgh* and HMS *Southampton* off Inchgarvie. Again Pinkerton attacked, blessing his luck that he should be so fortunate as to get two cracks at the enemy in one day, and to his great satisfaction, down went a Junker 88, spiralling into the sea off Crail.

A short time earlier, however, the radio message from a German reconnaissance plane to the approaching bombers had been intercepted and interpreted and the Spitfires of 603 (City of Edinburgh) Squadron of the Royal Auxiliary Air Force were also scrambled. Flight Lieutenant Denholm and Pilot Officers Gilroy and Morton went out on the hunt. A Heinkel was spotted east of Dalkeith and it was 'tallyho' once more as 603 Squadron went into the attack and shot down the raider to hit the sea near Port Seton. It gave 603 Squadron the distinction and glory of claiming the first enemy plane of the war to be shot down over Britain. In the same action they also engaged a Heinkel over Rosyth and another east of Aberdour, but were unable to claim 'kills'.

On the ground, there was consternation in Edinburgh streets and almost as much excitement as up in the clouds. Bullets had struck several buildings in the city, including the Joppa home of Lord Provost Sir Henry Steele. Even

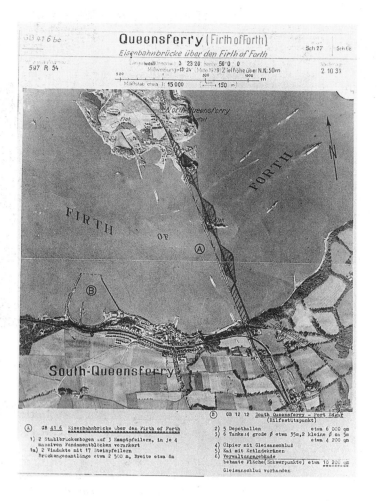

67, 68 & 70. Before the outbreak of war, the *Luftwaffe* had, with typical Teutonic efficiency, photographed most the strategic targets in the country. These are aerial photographs of the Firth of Forth (with the rail bridge clearly marked), Granton Harbour and the RAF field at Turnhouse.

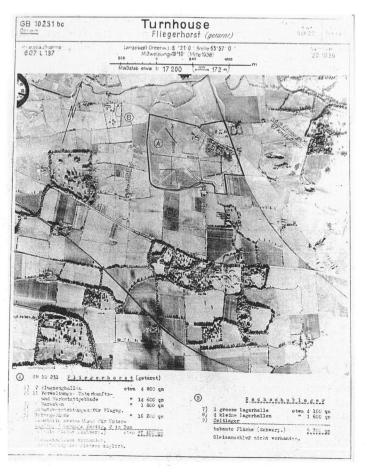

71. *above:* September 1939 and pilots of 602 (City of Glasgow) Squadron pictured shortly after their successful Firth of Forth action.

72. *left:* Full honours at the funeral in Portobello Cemetery of two German airmen as men of the RAF bear the coffins.

73. *below:* The German bomber downed in East Lothian following the Firth of Forth action on 28 October 1939. The aircraft is a Heinkel III dive bomber.

more disturbing, two people had been hit. Edinburgh was not expecting such an audacious attack by day and there were no shortages of eyewitnesses and opinions about the thrilling air battle high above the city. The Chief Constable's down-to-earth official report provides the best description of the Capital's first-hand experience of a memorable dog fight: "About 2.40 pm the sound of gunfiring and bursting shells was clearly heard in the city and puffs of white smoke were seen towards the west. As no warning of an air-raid had been received by 2.45 pm, I telephoned the district commissioner's office asking for information. They in turn inquired from the regional commissioner's office as to the reason for the firing. At about 2.50 pm I received a telephone message from the district commissioner's office to the effect that an air-raid had taken place on warships at South Queensferry, but that the raid was over.

"Injuries: a man of thirty-one years, while at work in the military camp at West Pilton, was struck on the leg by a machine gun bullet. He was taken by a passing car to the Western General Hospital where he is to undergo an operation to have the bullet removed.

"A man, whilst working in a garden at Portobello, was struck on the right side by a machine gun bullet and was removed to Leith Hospital by police ambulance, where he is to have an immediate operation, the bullet having lodged near to the stomach.

"Damage: twelve premises, including the Northern General Hospital and Granton Gas Works, were struck by bullets and shell fragments, resulting in broken windows, punctured roofs, etc."

The day was not yet over. Word arrived that a convoy was being bombed by a Heinkel near St Abb's Head. Once more 603 Squadron went to the rescue. The attack by the Spitfires hit the Heinkel hard. It attempted to make for home, but the pilot found his plane too badly damaged so he turned back then crashed. The squadron sprinted to base for a fast re-fuel before returning to guide HMS *Gurkha* to the spot where three of the four-man crew were afloat in a dinghy. They were taken prisoner and brought to Edinburgh for interrogation.

Historically, it was the first confrontation of the war over Britain as well as being a considerable triumph and the

74. A landmine dropped by parachute caused this extensive damage to David Kilpatrick's School, Leith, 7 April 1941.

exploits of these young auxiliary pilots were widely proclaimed. Not only was it a morale-booster to the country as it waited apprehensively for the first German bombs, it was also an impressive display of RAF derring-do by part-time pilots — "those long-haired, weekend amateur fliers" — who had reassuringly demonstrated to Britain, and given warning to the *Luftwaffe*, that we were prepared.

> "One of my memories of the war years was that our upstairs neighbour's son was shot down. He was in an open boat for days before he was rescued. He eventually made his way home and arrived with three bananas, all that was left of a big bunch. He gave one to his mother, one to his sister and I got the other one. I hardly knew how to eat it. We eventually hung up the skin on a piece of string so that neighbours could come along and sniff it. We had quite a queue."
> *Former Dunkeld Resident*

75. *right:* Flt Lt Pat Gifford with his Spitfire aircraft nicknamed "Stickleback" after claiming the first "kill" of the war: the German bomber he shot down on its raid over the Forth was the first to be shot down on British soil. He recorded in his diary: "Got a Hun over Port Seton."

76. Pilots of 603 (City of Edinburgh) Squadron at the beginning of the war. At this time they were on Forth area patrol.

The message went out to Germany: "Do your worst — we're ready!"

There was considerable competition between 602 and 603 Squadrons, the old Glasgow and Edinburgh rivalries once again asserting themselves, but on 28 October they shared another notable 'first'. A Heinkel III was engaged and hit by 602 Squadron and 603 swooped to finish it off. It crash-landed on the moor at Kidlaw, six miles south of Haddington, and VIPs came from far and near to inspect the remains of what was the first German plane to be shot down onto mainland Britain. Both squadrons distinguished themselves during the Battle of Britain and 603 accounted for seven Italian Fiat CR42 biplanes — the Italians' first and only venture into British skies.

Clydeside was clearly such a strategically important focus that it could not long escape the attentions of the *Luftwaffe*. More and more of the foreign-going vessels, which were taking such a pummelling in the English ports, were directed northwards to the Clyde, ensuring that the whole area became a compelling target for the German bomber command. Although Scotland suffered considerably less than London and some other English cities, Glasgow nonetheless was singled out for bombing runs by the *Luftwaffe*, with the first night raid taking place on 18 September 1939, when George Square in the centre of town was hit. It is the 'bomber moon' nights of 13 and 14 March 1941, however, that are most remembered: the nights Clydebank was blitzed.

The first sticks of bombs fell just after 9.30 pm, small ones at first to drive the people into their shelters, then came the incendiaries to torch the way for the 'big stuff'. The pattern was well-tested and targets were quickly floodlit as first Singer's timber yard and Yoker Distillery went up in a blaze of writhing flame and sparks. Then John Brown's shipyard, the Royal Ordnance Factory at Dalmuir and three Admiralty oil tanks helped to light the path for the raiders. As the bomber waves passed over largely without opposition, shedding their loads, it was time for the firefighters to move in and it was quickly realised that their task was on a scale outside their comprehension.

77. *above:* The remains of a twin-engined Wellington bomber which landed on a semi-detached bungalow in Craiglockhart View, Edinburgh. Five members of the crew were killed. Fortuitously, there were no civilian casualties.

78. *below:* UXB. An army bomb disposal unit searches for a German bomb on Auchencorth Moss, south of Penicuik, Midlothian. It was widely believed that a raider was trying to hit the ammunition dump at nearby Lamancha, where naval shells and other ammunition were stored beside the old railway line. Some of the sheds from those days are still standing and it is possible that unexploded bombs are still buried in the moor to this day.

—AND HERE ARE THREE OF THE MEN WHO TRIED TO BOMB THE FORTH BRIDGE

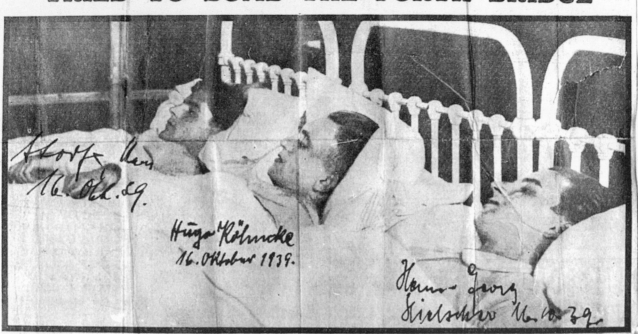

80. Over a million gallons of whisky were destroyed when a German bomb hit a bonded store in Dalry Road, Gorgie, Edinburgh, on 29 September 1940.

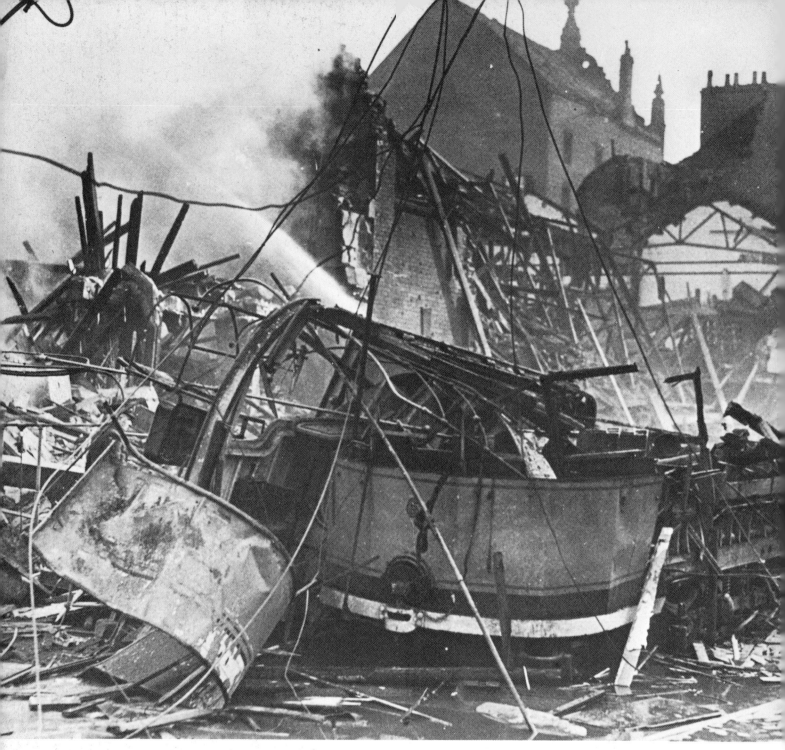

81. *above:* This Glasgow tram received a direct hit in Nelson Street on 17 March 1941.

82 & 83. *opposite page:* The morning after the first night of the Clydebank Blitz. The devastation within the relatively small area of Clydebank was almost total.

"The day after the Clydeside Blitz I was travelling from Glasgow to Dundee to join my ship. We were having a cuppa in the cafeteria in the old St Enochs Station at the top of Buchanan Street when a lorry crashed its gears at the top of the hill with a loud noise and half the people in the place dived under the tables. Glasgow was still jittery after the night before."
Glasgow Resident

"I remember the searchlights criss-crossing the sky above Glasgow and the sound of guns and bangs and the sky lighting up orange and flickering. I don't think I was really frightened."
Glasgow Health Worker

84. Rescue party at the scene of the Maryhill tenement which received a direct hit on the night of 14 March 1941. The scene was sketched by police "Special" and artist Ian Fleming in his police notebook and was later worked up into this etching and an oil painting.

85. Salvaging personal possessions after the Clydebank Blitz of March 1941.

"We knew something awful had happened", said an eye witness. "In the morning there were calls for anyone with a vehicle to get down there to see if they could be of help. I will never forget the sight: tenements reduced to rubble; people still in their nightclothes trying to salvage bits and pieces of belongings; some buildings still smoking, others on fire; people tearing at the bricks, shouting to try to discover survivors; prams, furniture, pots and pans, linen and toys scattered everywhere. I remember on my way down passing people heading into a reception area still in their nightdresses and men still in pyjamas. They looked haggard, some kids asleep over their mother's shoulder. There wasn't a smile among them. Some people's faces were still dirty from the smoke. I thought, my God, it's just like the pictures of refugees we'd seen on the newsreels and in the papers from Belgium and France, only it's here in Glasgow. It was unbelievable."

The toll over the two nights was in excess of 1,200 people killed. The official figures reported 528 had died in Clydebank. At least 2,000 had been injured. Only seven homes out of a housing stock of 12,000 houses were undamaged; 35,000 people out of a population of 47,000 were homeless.

The second night of the Blitz was less costly in lives and around 50 people died. Perhaps the lesson had been learned the hard way and more went to the shelters. Some simply seemed magically to vanish overnight to friends or relatives, while others made for the safety of the hills outside the town. Yet within a month many of those industries shattered by the raiders, including John Browns, were as busy as ever and returning to normal. Whatever the structural damage caused by those two nights of bombing terror it had certainly not affected the morale of the Clydesiders, and the deaths of those friends and neighbours in that compact shipbuilding town seemed merely to toughen resolve.

In May a further major air attack on the Clyde took place. This time Greenock, Gourock and Dumbarton were the targets. Although the Germans possessed detailed aerial maps of all strategic bombing zones in Scotland, a simulated town of canvas and wood had been created on the moors outside Dumbarton as a decoy. After the first bomber wave had passed in the now well-recognised pattern on the night of 5 May, fires were lit in the fake town to give the follow-on waves the impression that the town was well alight. Later it was discovered the ruse had worked well and around

86. Stonelaw School, Rutherglen, damaged in an air-raid in 1941.

ninety craters were found on the moors while only twenty bombs had landed on Dumbarton itself. Unfortunately, on the other side of the river Greenock lost 280 people that dreadful night along with a thousand homes.

Serious as they were, these raids turned out to be preliminaries before the main assault on the night of 7 May. A concentrated and relentless attack involving more than 200 German bombers struck Greenock once more, pounding the town until large swathes were left levelled or burning. A thousand homes were destroyed entirely and out of a total housing stock of 18,000 almost 10,000 homes were damaged. Cathcart Square was rubble, Lamont's drydock, the Walker's and Westburn sugar refineries and the Ingleston Street distillery took direct hits. The whole town shook and to observers from the opposite bank it seemed as if all Greenock was aflame and that nothing could survive. Although the two nights of carnage on Clydebank tend to be remembered as the most vicious air raids in Scotland, the little town of Greenock took more than its share.

The league table of bombs dropped on Scotland shows that 441 fell on Clydebank, 218 on Glasgow, 216 on Aberdeen and 187 on Greenock; Edinburgh, which did not seem to be a *Luftwaffe* priority, had 47 high explosive missiles dropped from 14 raids leaving 18 dead and 212 injured. By contrast, Aberdeen had 178 people killed in 34 raids. They tended to be hit-and-run encounters rather than the heavily-concentrated attacks suffered on the Clyde, but they generated their own kind of fear because citizens never knew when death and destruction would suddenly fall from the sky. The Silver City was kept in a constant state of tautness.

In April 1943 came Aberdeen's blackest night when twenty-five Dorniers struck the north of the city killing 98 people. The most satisfying moment had been in July 1940, when a determined Heinkel III on a solo daylight mission was shot down over Rosemount and crashed where the ice rink now stands on South Anderson Drive. Unfortunately, before it met its end a trail of havoc had been left across the city, including a direct hit on the boiler house at Hall Russell's. Marischal Street and King Street also took hits and several people lost their lives.

Aberdeen was Scotland's most frequently raided city and as the war progressed its citizens were not unaccustomed on their way to work to seeing sudden alterations to its look as whole buildings disappeared or were left in ruins. In fact, the whole of the North East was on the receiving end of Hitler's bombers and even Peterhead and Fraserburgh were given a hard time. When the raids eventually ceased Fraserburgh had taken 87 bombs with the loss of 49 lives and many injured; Peterhead received eleven bombs less with a death toll of 38. Dundee got off lightly, and often the bombs dropped along Tayside were Germans simply off-loading before heading out across the sea to their bases, although Montrose came in for a period of repeated raids without apparent reason.

87. Bomb crater at the corner of Dalkeith Road and Nesbitt Street, Dundee, after the raid of September 1940.

88. The scene at Cathcart Street, Greenock, May 1941.

89. Rosefield Street, Dundee, after the raid of September 1940.

90. Bomb damage at 55 Wellington Road, Torry, Aberdeen, 4 November 1940.

"My old grandad had been in the HLI in the First World War. We all had great respect for him and we used to listen to his stories. On the night of the Clydeside Blitz a bomb came down quite near us and the whole house shook. My grandfather shouted in a voice I had never heard before: 'Get down, get down! All of you. Eat the carpet!' Grandad was in charge again. We obeyed."
Former Clydebank Resident

"I remember being on guard duty at Stobbs camp in the dead of winter. I was frozen stiff. I remember thinking that if I can survive Stobbs I can survive anything. And I came marching home at the end of the war intact."
Former Royal Scots Fusilier

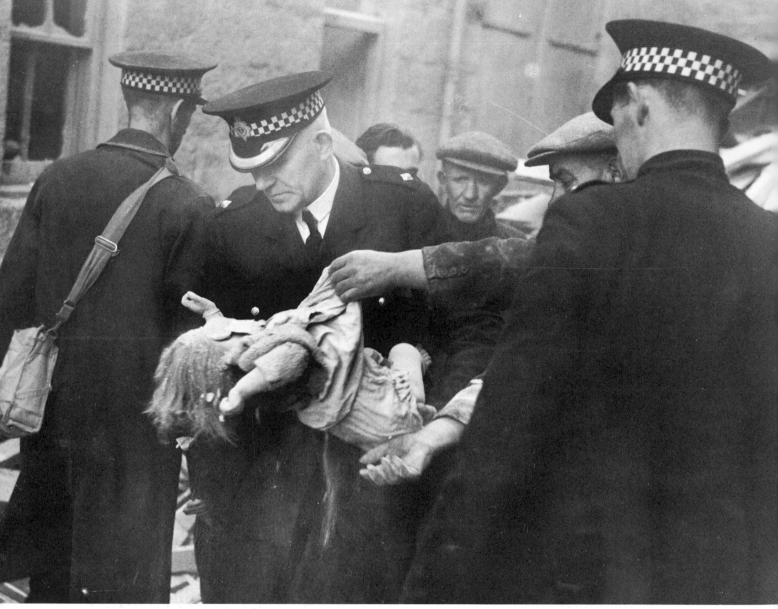

91. A young survivor of an attack on Peterhead, 29 September 1940.

WATCH OUT FOR THIS!

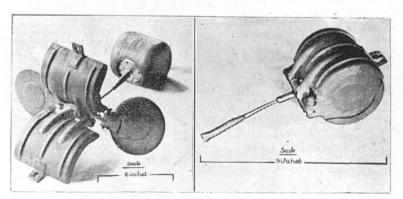

The new German anti-personnel bomb, which has been dropped over Britain in recent raids. Weighing about 4 lbs, and usually painted either greyish-green or a bright yellow, the bomb is liable to explode easily. The public are warned not to touch or approach such a bomb, but to report it to the nearest warden or police officer. The bomb, which the authorities state resembles a large round cigarette tin and has a short thick wire protruding from one side, may be found with the casing open (left) or shut (right.)

"I spent a few months in Cullen during the war when I was a boy. It used to be great for beachcombing along the foot of the cliffs. My mother warned me off the beach because the debris of war was constantly being washed up. There was always the danger of mines and bombs, but to a fourteen year old it was a great adventure. One day I found an airman's leather flying helmet which became the envy of my pals. Unfortunately, my mother later found it in my cupboard. What a scene there was when it came out I had been down to the beach. She was very upset. Eventually she calmed down and said did I not realise that it probably belonged to some poor airman who had been shot down and remember that Uncle Tommy was in aircrew. I didn't go back to the beach for years."

Aberdeen Resident

93. Workmen extricate a cleansing department lorry from debris after Aberdeen's Poynerhook Road depot was seriously damaged, 6 August 1941.

94. Bomb damage to Peterhead Academy, 20 July 1940.

95. *opposite page:* The Music Hall on Aberdeen's Union Street dramatically decorated for Salute the Soldier Week, May 1944.

"You always knew when they were German planes because they had a different kind of engine sound. It was a kind of droning wow-wow-wow. Once, to our consternation, we saw a German 'flying pencil' above Brechin. It was low and you could see the crosses. What a shock. We all crouched down in the bracken."
Dundee Resident

The Home Front

Although the fighting, the victories and the reverses dominated the headlines in war time press, the vast majority of the population ws engaged in enduring an often dull and repetitive regime brought about by rationing, blackout and shortages. So many things were happening so fast that newspapers hardly had enough space to publish anything other than war news and information. Getting around in the blackout was proving a real hazard in itself and, in spite of having shielded sidelights and traffic lights, accident figures went soaring. It was estimated that around one in five people were involved in blackout mishaps of one kind or another, most of them not serious, but a few dramatic and fatal. To try to help matters, road obstacles were painted white and white bands appeared on car running boards and bumpers, but there was so much activity that the roads — as well as pavements — had never been busier or more dangerous.

Torches were quickly sold out and a kind of blind-man's-buff or follow-the-leader game took place nightly as a single file of fellow-travellers tried to find their way homewards behind someone who knew where they were going or who surreptitiously held a dimmed torch. No one dared breach the blackout code and run the gauntlet of an abrasive voice shouting "Put out that light!" It became so difficult for road users to steer their vehicles in the blackout that by October Glasgow tram drivers decided they would not operate after 8.00 pm. It wasn't a strike, they stressed, it was just impossible.

The first petrol rationing of 150 miles a month lifted pressure off the roads for a while; but troops were pouring in from around the world, factories were being built, camps were being erected, servicemen were trying to reach their regiments, and bases or ships and military manoeuvres seemed to be everywhere. The government took over the main railway companies and the troops virtually took over the trains, which often ran late because of air-raids, breakdowns, lack of spare parts or hold-ups on the line.

Bus companies were short of petrol, staff, spares and vehicles. But there was a tremendous spirit of make-do-and-mend to keep the country moving. Throughout the war in Scotland transport staff came out with great credit. Eventually, only doctors, farmers and other essential workers were allowed petrol, car output ground to a halt and existing cars were garaged away to be produced for bargain hunters when hostilities were finally over.

Rationing! Everyone knew it was coming and dreaded the moment. Sugar, butter and eggs were the foods that most people felt they would miss. Inevitably there was some stowing away and when clothes, furniture and other commodities were also rationed or in short supply, a busy blackmarket trade flourished in the cities. In country areas the same hardships were not experienced and farm butter and eggs were freely available if you knew where to go. Some country folk even resorted to keeping bees as an increased sugar ration was required to feed them.

Basically, rationing was introduced to ensure fair shares for all. Although some items were not rationed it did not mean they were immediately obtainable: the children's delights of bananas and ice cream disappeared quickly to return only at the end of the war; restaurants were forbidden to offer meals costing more than five shillings; and fish and eggs were in short supply depending where you lived. But there was never a shortage of potatoes and bread, which

97. Milk, cheese, flour, butter, sugar, margarine, bacon, lard, jam, meat and tea: enough for one whole week under wartime regulations.

98. This horse-drawn cart operated by Glasgow Corporation Cleansing Department advertised the virtues of saving kitchen waste for feeding to pigs.

99. Everyday documents for a wartime civilian population.

"I remember there was a bunch of imitation bananas in this grocer's shop which had been used as an advertisement before the war. I was only a child and had never seen a real banana; I used to pester my mother to tell me how it tasted; she tried to explain but it is virtually impossible to describe the taste of a banana and that only made me even more curious. Well, I never found out until the war was over. During the early part of the war *Oor Willie* and the *Beano* used to have people slipping on banana skins and I wondered where they got them. By the end of the war they were slipping on orange peel."

Edinburgh Teacher

100. Rubber, which had to be imported on the long and perilous sea route, was in short supply and recycling was seen as the answer. This was a Glasgow Corporation Cleansing Department Thames cab and trailer.

were often proffered in ingenious forms under exotic names to help keep nutritional boredom to a minimum.

In the summer of 1940 Government nutritionists proposed that the people of Britain could healthily survive on twelve ounces of bread, a pound of potatoes, two ounces of oatmeal, an ounce of fat, six ounces of vegetables and six-tenths of a pint of milk per day, with either an additional small measure of cheese, meat, fish, sugar, eggs, dried milk or a little more of the same. This proposal had been drawn up with the worst possible war scenario in mind of Britain being besieged by U-boats and supply lines being cut. But Churchill, who prided himself on being a trencherman as well as enjoying his other creature comforts, decided the country had not reached that dire situation and that such a step would be detrimental to morale. The idea was, therefore, mercifully buried to be resurrected only in extreme situations, and there were sighs of relief all round.

Nonetheless ration books were issued in January 1940, with butter, sugar (eight ounces) and bacon (four ounces) first on the list as expected. Meat followed in March, tea in July and jam, marmalade, syrup and cheese early in 1941. A points scheme was then introduced so that as well as paying cash each person also had a certain number of points to spend in a week, and the Ministry of Food could regulate the points according to the availability of supply. It was a measure that made sense because until that time it was too easy to direct unrationed goods to those who had an ability to pay, rather than need, and it made the lives of the blackmarketeers much more difficult.

The ladies of the Larkhall-Dalserf Women's Voluntary Service went as far as producing their own hardbacked *Thrift Cookery Book*, price 2s 6d, as part of their war effort to get the best out of what was available. Anne McNay, the organiser, along with Lady Ruth Balfour, chairman of the Scottish WVS, pointed out that not only was it an attempt to educate people about food values at a time of shortages

but also to preserve that good old Scottish custom of thrift in the kitchen and home generally.

Ways with Raw Fats offered one suggestion; *Ways with Scraps of Cooked Fat* volunteered another. There was the advice that if potatoes were peeled raw then waste was incurred at the rate of about a quarter of a pound in every pound. "Always boil them in their jackets", counsels the book. Housewives back from a hard day in the munitions factory were offered recipes on how to utilise stale bread in liver dumplings and stale bread puddings; ways to use up sour milk; mock duck, curried rabbit, fried pike, and lentil rissoles; milk, bone, pea, kail and potato soups; and, of course, the haggis himself. Today, some of these offerings appear bizarre, although many of the recipes in the book provided Scots with a healthy and balanced diet for years. It was also a demonstration, however, that Scotland was ready to tighten its belt and prepare for the worst. Over at the BBC at 8.15 am each morning from Monday to Friday further helpful advice was dispensed from the wartime *Kitchen Front*.

Although it was a time of unremitting cutbacks everywhere, the Government caught the country by surprise with a social reform "of the first magnitude": cheap or free milk was provided to mothers and small children. It was delivered mostly to schools ready for playtime and a solemn, concentrated, welcome gurgling took place in classrooms throughout the land. Similarly, it was felt that some manual workers such as miners should also be kept in trim and they were allowed a little more cheese for their 'pieces'.

Mostly, however, it was a tale of austerity as one by one items which had been taken for granted

101. Liberton Scouts and Guides load a home-made camp trailer with salvaged jam jars. Along with pots and pans, old newspapers and empty food cans, jam jars were collected for recycling in aid of the war effort. In practice, much of the salvaged material was quite worthless and its value was ultimately more psychological in nature.

102. Ration book distribution in Edinburgh.

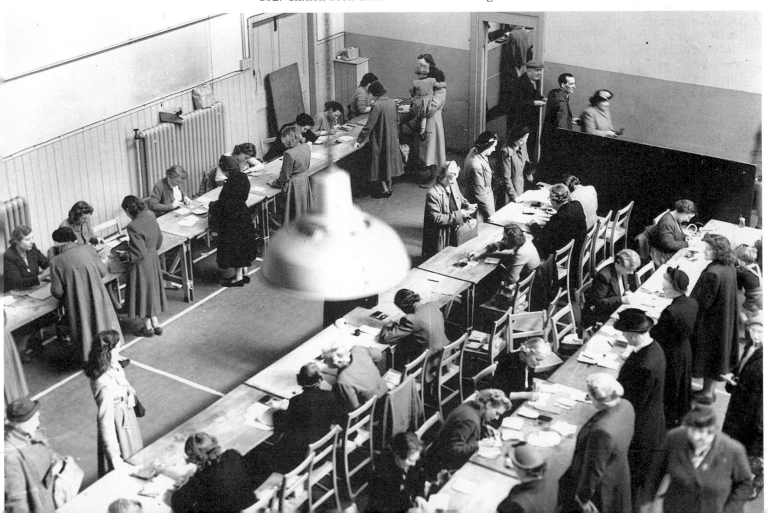

104. *right:* Down on the farm there was much to be done — especially at harvest time. Here, on a farm near Duns, women and Italian prisoners of war work side by side with the more regular local labour. 105. *opposite page:* Ammunition girls at Aberdeen Munitions Factory, April 1941.

began to disappear or became more difficult to obtain as the war effort took priority. The Limitation of Supplies Order in the summer of 1940, for example, cut back the production of seventeen types of goods ranging from toys to jewellery and knives and forks. So it continued until the last rationing measures of the war took place in 1942, with soap limited to sixteen ounces for every four-week period and chocolate and sweets to twelve ounces in four weeks.

In the main, people accepted it all willingly. There were complaints, of course, but some measures which at first glance appeared petty and excessive were seen in the end to make sense, ensuring that the right resources went to the right places in the cause of the war effort. At one period it looked as if men would have to grow whiskers, such was the shortage of razor blades. Utility suits did nothing for the male figure and a shortage of cosmetics was inevitably criticised by women.

It was an offence to feed pets with food which could be consumed by humans but the introduction of dried eggs and powdered 'Household Milk', which caused more quips than complaints, resulted in many families having exceedingly well-nurtured cats and dogs! Nationally, wheatmeal bread as a substitute for white bread created furious debate and it was frequently and rudely suggested what the Government could do with it. Cigarettes and beer, the working man's pleasures, were never rationed, although there were times when the water content of a pint reached record levels of dilution. Common sense and the odd moan overcame the shortages, and the nation was probably fitter as a result. In perspective it was recognised that less sugar and the lack of bananas was a small price to pay when set against the toll in merchant seamen's lives.

If there had been a 'Phoney War' for land forces it was unknown to the Navy who had been plunged into nervy, hot war from the outset. The relentless U-boat attacks ensured that Britain's imports were substantially reduced, which in turn meant more had to be produced from the land at home. Agricultural production had declined before the war, but now it became an essential element of the survival plan. The Land Girls, all 5,500 of them in Scotland, the majority of whom had never held a shovel in earnest and had previously even steered well clear of cows in a field, set to work with a will on the multitude of tasks that is part and parcel of the hard work of farm life. Such was the drive for output that on occasions even troops were used, along with schoolchildren, at harvest periods to get in the crops. An Irish labour force, which had to check in regularly with the police as a security precaution, grew in numbers until there were around 3,500 of them and as the war continued German and Italian prisoners, with distinctive big round patches on their backs, were also set to work in the fields.

By 1944 100,000 men and women worked for the Ministry of Aircraft Production: new or repaired Merlin engines were produced at the Rolls Royce factory at Hillington, the biggest single undertaking in Scotland, which employed 25,000 at its peak; the Blackburn Aircraft Company at Dumbarton built the twin-engined reconnaissance bomber, the Botha, and later built Sunderland four-engined flying-boats; in the early years at Prestwick the army reconnaissance Lysander was built; the dismantled Cairn shipyard in Greenock was converted by Scottish Aviation into a flying-boat factory; Ardeer, in Ayrshire, made explosives; every kind of bomb, including the big ten tonners, were made in an area between Lanarkshire and Falkirk; in Glasgow's Kelvin Hall 1,000

106. *above:* Inside the Rolls Royce factory Foundry Section at Hillington, near Glasgow.

108. *right:* Edinburgh girl Mary Lusher smartly turned out in her Women's Land Army uniform. She worked on estates and farms around Lilliesleaf in the Borders.

107. *below:* Assembling Merlin engine parts at Hillington.

109. A section of the Women's Timber Corps on parade in the City Square, Dundee, June 1943.
110. Women's Land Army girls parade on Princess Street, Edinburgh.

women toiled to make 6,500 barrage balloons and 20,000 rescue dinghies. In Fort William, the aluminium used for making aircraft was manufactured, and rolling mills were constructed at Falkirk; the Stirling Gas Company produced hydrogen for the barrage balloons and material to be used for explosives; in Kirkcaldy the linoleum companies were involved in making aircraft; ships were being prefabricated inland then brought to the coast for building and small towns that had never dreamt of having a shipyard suddenly also found themselves caught up in the frenzy of the war effort.

The list of activity lengthened and spread throughout the whole country. Transporting heavy goods was a major task and so new railway stations were built at Garnock East, Garnock West, Powfoot (Annan) and Grangestone (Girvan). Just like that! Nothing was to hold up the war effort. The new stations and trains needed manpower to staff them, and manpower was in short supply. But in wartime Scotland womanpower was playing a vital role as the petticoat army took over much of what had formerly been recognised as the preserve of men; by the middle of 1943 around 40 per cent of the country's workforce were women.

Scotland had never known a time of such dramatic, far-reaching change, so many new experiences and so many confusing as well as exciting situations. The war touched every city, every village, every individual. But after the painful slump years of the Thirties Scotland was also put to work. Factories were being opened, particularly for munitions. Whatever the need, that national spirit in the face of adversity ensured it was tackled at the double. It was not only munitions that demanded manpower: the need to increase coal output was also paramount and the call for more miners became a national priority which continued for the duration of the war. Even in 1944, when the requirements of the armed forces were at their height, one in every ten call-ups between the ages of eighteen and twenty-five were directed down the mines. They were the celebrated 'Bevin Boys', named after Ernest Bevin, the Minister of Labour, who devised the scheme.

Gradually, as the war progressed, all the training, all the armed forces united from around the world, all the effort that went into winning the war at the battlefront began to pay dividends. But there was obviously more to achieving

111. Assembling Lee Enfield rifles in Morris's former Milton Street furniture factory, Glasgow.

112. Inside the air-raid shelter at Duncan's chocolate factory, Canonmills, Edinburgh (1941).

In 1942, His Majesty the late King George VI inspected the works and in company with the Queen and senior officers watched a drive past of completed tanks to the testing ground. Their Majesties discussed items of interest with the workmen concerned. The Queen asked one of the apprentices (below) what he was making and the delighted youngster blushingly answered 'Time-and-a-hauf, mum!'

HIS MAJESTY KING GEORGE VI VISITS THE WORKS

114. During the war, Glasgow's North British Locomotive Company remained one of the city's biggest employers. Railway engines were still made alongside tanks and armoured vehicles.

victory than mere production of weaponry, superior forces or political or military leadership. On the Home Front it was the people's war that counted and the people responded not just with the endeavour and fortitude that could be expected of them in the circumstances, but with such determination, such vitality and passion — just as Churchill wanted — that somehow the possibility of being on the losing side was almost inconceivable. Amidst the bombs, the fears, the scares, the drudgery, the disasters, the terrible toll of personal loss, the whole bewildering upheaval of war, a sense of mission developed, accelerating quickly to something resembling exhilaration in the war effort.

Whether it was in the munitions factories, with the Land Girls on the farms, trying to fulfil the Government's plea to Make-Do-and-Mend in the Home, Digging for Victory, organising for Warship Week, Spitfire Week, Wings for Victory Week, Red Cross comforts, defeating Squander Bug, supporting campaigns like Help Scotland's Harvest or the direct appeal to women to 'Come Into the Factories', whatever the activity, it was pursued with commitment and fervour. Slave hard, play hard, let's have a laugh; tomorrow is another day, and who knows what the next will bring. Live

for the moment and don't think too deeply about the war or it could drive you round the bend. Many people did think too long and deeply about the war because they suffered grievous loss. But in the main the grief was silent and in private, as it had to be, and a different, cheerier face was presented for public consumption. Whether or not many people on the Home Front actually formulated these thoughts, it was nonetheless exactly how it was.

The war was not joyless. People laughed a lot, they danced and went to the cinema a lot, they sang a lot — *Run, Rabbit, Run, In the Quartermaster's Stores, Roll out the Barrel, Bless 'em All, Mairzy Doats and Dozy Dotes, Praise the Lord and Pass the Ammunition, I'll Be Seeing You, You Are My Sunshine, The Toorie on his Bonnet*. Some of it was inane, but it was a laugh and the world was mad anyway. They sought humour, turned the serious into a snigger and the funny into a guffaw. Large helpings were served directly to them: Tommy Handley kept them laughing in radio's *ITMA* (*It's That Man Again*) along with his cronies Colonel Chinstrap, Mrs Mopp, Funf, the German spy, and Ali Oop. Vic Oliver, Bebe Daniels and Ben Lyon kept them laughing. There was Wilfred Pickles and Cyril Fletcher, Harry Lauder,

115. *left:* The war meant that women took on all sorts of hitherto unknown roles. This cheerful group from Edinburgh became truck drivers ferrying loads down to England.

116. *below:* The WVS serve up the tea at Waverley Station.

117. *opposite page, top left:*Food economy was widely advised — and practised.

118. *opposite page, top right:* Servicemen enjoy a cuppa at Perth Station.

119. *opposite page, middle:* The canteen at the Scottish Rest House for Servicemen, Waterloo Place, Edinburgh.

120. *opposite page, bottom left:* Take a walk . . .

121. *opposite page, bottom right:* A Mrs Bailey serves tea and hot pies to servicemen at Perth Station. The war meant that at any one time many thousands of soldiers, airmen and sailors were on the move and had to be refreshed.

> "My wife and daughter came to Perth Station to see me off in the train. We all felt miserable. No one knew what the future held. I didn't know if I would ever be back. We waved to each other as the train left the platform until we all just tiny figures. Then suddenly the train stopped. After a moment it slowly shunted back into the Station on the next platform. Consternation! My wife was crying and my daughter was laughing. Having said our goodbyes and then seeing each other both again was almost too much to bear. I jumped back out of the train and we all went home. I caught an early train the next day and nobody said anything."
>
> *Former RAOC Sergeant*

Jack Radcliffe, Tommy Morgan, Jack Anthony and Dave Willis in his "wee gas mask" had them holding their sides; and Vera Lynn supplied the necessary nostalgia. It was with a laugh that the people overcame.

In their view, if they thought about it at all, it was neither particularly clever, heroic or patriotic. Simply they overcame because they wanted to. It was spontaneous, matter-of-fact, the job to be done — and it was infectious. It was the way things were. In Scotland ordinary people began to throw off the inhibitions of years; they moved or were directed to different parts of the country and even the world. For many it was an eye-opener. Suddenly they were faced with a whole new — and exciting — range of experiences. Some were mundane, others traumatic, but they changed people's lives. Even in war there were opportunities: because of war opportunities presented themselves and, as with an open door, people passed through to see what was on the other side. Along with the agonies on the other side there were also new horizons.

To look back on those grim early war headlines it seems extraordinary that there was scope for laughter or aspiration:

May 1940. The dark days after the evacuation of Dunkirk, the fall of St Valery, where the prime of the 51st Highland Division is forced to surrender as the French capitulate and Britain stands alone against a German army that seems invincible (it is then that the first emotional wave of public support declares itself in the welcome to our 338,000 troops as they return in a variety of small boats from the beaches of Dunkirk in that remarkable escape); on the Home Front Britain digs in and prepares for invasion; the newspaper headlines are breath-catching as fraught actions are reported from the battlefronts; the front line in the air as our pilots fight the Battle of Britain along the South Coast; the war at sea as both the Royal and the Merchant Navy take on the U-boats and dive-bombers in the Battle of the Atlantic; the war in the deserts of North Africa.

1941. Touch-and-go for survival. Our cities, particularly London, receive the full force of the blitz; Rommel and his Africa Korps launch their assault on British forces; Yugoslavia and Greece fall and the Germans invade Russia. A gleam of satisfaction as the *Bismark* is sunk; Rudolf Hess, Hitler's right hand man, parachutes into Scotland to meet the Duke of Hamilton, breaks an ankle, hirples off under arrest and a young reporter called Max McAuslane, later Editor of the *Edinburgh Evening News*, is first with the news. Pearl Harbour is bombed and America enters the war. The Japanese army makes inroads into South East Asia and Hong Kong is taken.

1942. The tide begins to turn. Although the Japanese continue to sweep through Asia and Singapore surrenders, Rommel makes gains in the desert; in Russia the Germans falter; the RAF begins its campaign of obliteration bombing; Commandos make a daring raid on the U-boat base at St Nazaire; Malta wins the George Cross; the Americans shock Tokyo with a surprise bombing run; Montgomery beats off Rommel at El Alamein and proceeds to 'hit him for six'; but

122. This enemy Messerschmit was sent for display in Dundee City Square as part of the savings campaign for Wings for Victory Week

123. Firefighting squad in decontamination gear, Duncan's chocolate factory, Edinburgh (1941).

the Dieppe raid is only partially successful and Britain sustains heavy losses.

1943. Off to an encouraging start as the Germans surrender at Stalingrad; the first day-time bombing of Berlin takes place by daring RAF Mosquitos, the mass bombing of the Ruhr strikes hard at German industry, and the 'Dambusters' breach the Mohne and Eder dams; the Africa Korps is on the run; the U-boats are at last on the receiving end; the Germans are smashed in the great tank battle at Kursk outside Moscow; the Allies land in Sicily; the Germans lose the *Scharnhorst*, their last major battleship; it is hopeful news everywhere and dreams of invading Europe are becoming a reality.

1944. The rout of the Germans continues with landings at Anzio and the intense bombing of Berlin; the Russians snap the siege line around Leningrad; the Americans make headway against the Japanese in the Pacific, the British jungle-fighters take the war to the Japanese in Burma; in Italy the advance pushes northwards, Monte Cassino is taken and Rome liberated; on 6 June the biggest invasion force in history, under General Dwight D Eisenhower, hits the beaches of Normandy and after fierce fighting the Allies break out; Paris is liberated amid scenes of joy; the first of the Nazi death camps is found in Poland; the airborne assault on Arnhem, which could have shortened the war, is a disaster with heavy casualties and prisoners taken; the bunting goes up in Athens to welcome the British return; the

last German cast of the die fails because of lack of supplies after an unexpected cut-and-thrust break-out in the Ardennes.

1945. Germany is being crushed. Berlin is under day and night aerial bombardment; the Allies cross the Rhine and close in; Berlin is left a shattered city of rubble as the Russians get there first; the Führer in his underground bunker, with all hope gone but continuing to direct imaginary armies, finally shoots himself; in Milan Mussolini is captured, executed with a machine gun burst and ignominiously strung up by the heels for all to see; a million Germans surrender to Field Marshal Alexander in Italy on 29 April; in a tent on Luneburg Heath on May 4 Field Marshal Montgomery accepts the surrender of all enemy forces in North-West Germany, Holland and Denmark; and at 2.41 am on 7 May General Eisenhower accepts the unconditional surrender terms from General Alfred Jodl, the German emissary. The war in Europe is over.

These were the headlines and many, many more that caught the eye as the war unfolded. There were more war horror stories to come before the Japanese surrender after the world heard in awe that atomic bombs had been dropped on Hiroshima and Nagasaki to foreshadow the shape of fear to come. But it was the end of the war in Europe that turned on the lights again and rang out the bells.

There had been plenty of time to prepare for the celebrations. As early as September 1944 floodlighting was

124. A Messerschmit 109, shot down in Kent, in the unlikely location of Princess Street Gardens. It launched the WVS Fighting Planes Fund of 1940. Third from the left is Lady Ruth Balfour, first Scottish President of the WVS.

125. A red letter day at the Middleton Evacuee Camp in Midlothian as chocolate-flavoured milk powder arrives, a gift from "The Kinsmens' Clubs of Canada" (1943).

"Dancing was all the rage in those wartime days. We girls used to get all dressed up, but unless you knew an American airman who had access to nylons you went along bare-legged to the dance wearing your liquid stocking out of a bottle. It was really only a brown stain that was painted or dabbed onto our legs and it fooled no one, but we used to draw seams down the back of each other's legs to make it look as if we had the real thing. I remember getting ready for a big Christmas dance in Kilmarnock with a special boyfriend and my young sister spilled my stockings when she was painting her own legs. She was about twelve at the time. I remember screaming that she had ruined my life."

Kilmarnock Resident

confidently being erected in Princes Street Gardens in Edinburgh ready for the victory party. As it turned out, when the time came there was an unexpected delay in the official announcement and many revellers just could not wait. Sporadic and impromtu advance celebrations began to break out all over the country. Flags, bunting, bonfires and street parties were everywhere.

Tuesday 8 May 1945 was VE Day. Theatre and cinema performances were interrupted to bring the news and throughout Scotland the people took to the streets. It was a time to do crazy things, to give in to the celebrations in entirety. After all, in the American parlance of the time, there could be no better reason for "having a ball". In Europe the fighting, the killing, the maiming were over. We had survived. We had fought the war we did not want. We had won. We were alive.We were free. Of course, there were official speeches and thanksgiving services saying all the right things, but for that moment thoughts were concentrated on having a party. And the partying went on for days — and nights — because it was time to let go all the pent-up emotions and stresses of nearly six years in one enormous, wonderful, ecstatic roar of relief and to shout "Thank God it's over."

There were crushes in all the city centres. Traffic came to a standstill. Crowds were laughing, hugging, kissing, singing, dancing, hooching, drinking, crying in ecstasy. Some could not stand the pace and were parked somewhere in blissful oblivion until found later by friends. One Canadian army sergeant unconsciously created a traffic jam of his own in Princes Street when he seraphically lay under a bush in the gardens, bottles by his side, while hundreds pressed to view and cheer him. Soldiers, sailors, airmen, Scots, English, Welsh, Irish, Americans, Australians, Canadians, New Zealanders, Poles, nurses, firemen, ARP, Home Guard, WVS, munitions workers, Land Girls, everyone from everywhere who had played a part linked arms with strangers in glorious peace. It happened again on VJ Day as a new Prime Minister, Mr Clement Atlee, announced that "the last of our enemies is laid low."

There were some who were not at the parties, but the mourning and account would come later.

127. *above:* Lunchtime for some of the day children at South Fort Street War-Time Nursery, Leith, the first Edinburgh Corporation residential war-time nursery. A little girl is seen bringing cups of milk to her companions: the children were encouraged in the art of self-sufficiency.

128. *opposite page:* Clydeside turned out the ships on a never-ending production line during the war.

129. A heavy AA battery marching along Castle Terrace to the old Caledonian railway station.

"I remember seeing my husband off for the last time at Dundee West Station. When I got back to the house I found half a cup of tea which was still warm and his cigarette stubs were in the ashtray. Tommy Handley was still on the radio. It was as if he was still there. I just sat down and cried."
Dundee Pensioner

130. Secretary of State for Scotland Tom Johnston makes the inspection of the Fire Service parade outside the
Royal Scottish Academy building, Edinburgh.

131. Lord Louis Mountbatten and his daughter Patricia at the launching of the aircraft carrier H M S *Indefatigable* on the Clyde, 1944.

132. Prime Minister Churchill with President Roosevelt's special envoy, Harry Hopkins, pictured on the historic visit to Glasgow in January 1941. On this visit Hopkins pledged US support for what was then Britain's lone stand.

133. Launch day at a Clydeside yard during the war. A section of the crowd.

134. Sir Harry Lauder addresses the crowd gathered for the launch.

135. *above:* General Montgomery visits the City Chambers, Glasgow, April 1944.

136. *right:* H M King George VI and Queen Elizabeth visit the Caledon Shipyard, Dundee.

137. Wartime funeral with full military honours, Piershill Cemetery, Edinburgh.

138. Glamour comes to the trams in Glasgow as women drivers take up their duties.

Friends and Foes

139. Two captured German flyers are escorted to the police station down Bell Street in Dundee. Their Heinkel was shot down over the city on a bombing mission.

The war brought a multitude of quite new experiences. For the first time ever, millions of Britons actually met foreigners and, in Scotland, there soon appeared the scattered remnants of foreign armies and air forces and prisoners of war from sunken naval and merchant ships and aircraft shot down on raids over the country.

Although Britain had gone to war in defence of the Poles, most Scots knew little about them or their country. Enormous sympathy for their plight and respect for their courage grew, however, as the Polish army was driven into Rumania and Hungary, their brave attempts to regroup in France brought to nothing when they were forced out again along with the British as that country fell to the German panzers. Most people in Scotland had never met or even seen a Pole, and there was fascination when they began to appear by the thousand.

For those who witnessed that first group arrive in Glasgow, twelve days after the French capitulation, it was a deeply moving experience. They were fair, good-looking young men — and some not so young — kitless, many in ill-fitting French army uniforms after their battlefront ordeals, but there was certainly nothing defeatist in their bearing. They marched smartly through Glasgow three abreast on their way to Holy Cross Church for a special mass. Soon a thousand voices were singing out Polish hymns, heartfelt as thoughts were concentrated on their ravished country and lost families and the miseries being endured back home. Glasgow folk have never been slow to rally round in such situations and, in spite of the language problems, they took the Polish soldiers and airmen to their hearts.

For a few days they were quartered at Hampden Park and Ibrox before dispersal to places like Abington, Biggar, Angus, Fife and Perthshire. Later they were allocated a defence sector on the Scottish coastline in case of German invasion. There was another occasion laden with emotion when General Sikorski, the charismatic Polish Commander-

"We went to war because Germany invaded Poland, but none of us had ever seen a Pole. Then the Polish soldiers arrived and we found that they were so polite and good looking. They had gold fillings in their teeth and they used to kiss the back of the ladies' hands. That was certainly something new in Scotland. And they had nice names, too, like Leon."

Glasgow Pensioner

140. This Polish infantry unit formed part of the east of Scotland defence forces and was photographed on manoeuvres. This photograph and the one below were subsequently issued as postcards.

141. Polish wireless infantry units in Scotland.

in-Chief, met his troops in Biggar and tied the blue and black ribbon of the *Virtuti Militari*, the Polish VC, to the standard of the Podhale Brigade for their valour at Narvic. With the curlews and peewits calling from the fields and moors around that little Border town, the General decorated his men, one of whom had wiped out two German machine-gun positions single-handed and lost a leg — all on his seventeenth birthday.

Wherever they went the Poles made friends, especially with children who quickly learned to greet them with a cheery "Dzien dobry" (good morning) or "dobry Wieczor" (good evening) and their genteel manners certainly struck a chord with Scots girls, many of whom married their Polish boyfriend soldiers and settled down with their new families after the war. Many learned English with a Glasgow accent after that city provided 40 teachers and, while waiting for re-equipment, hundreds of promising young Polish pupils took the *Duz Matura*, the equivalent of university matriculation. The Scottish universities co-operated in providing facilities for a Polish medical school with the power to confer its own degrees, for even then the Poles nurtured dreams of rebuilding their devastated country, and there would be a need for doctors, teachers, scientists and men of learning and vision. As it turned out, that dream has had a somewhat different ending to that envisaged in Scotland by General Haller, the Polish Minister of Education at the time.

The Norwegians arrived heroically in little groups. Some believed they were the only refugee survivors from the North Sea after landing far-scattered in small boats along the Aberdeenshire coast and as far north as Shetland. All shared the single objective of re-organising and re-arming so that they could return to free their homeland. They concentrated in Dumfries, where their ranks swelled as Norwegians from around the world — even long-voyage whalers on the return journey — answered their country's plea for help. King Haakon, himself exiled and determined to win back his throne, visited his Viking Army, as he called them affectionately, and spoke of their heritage and the need to return it safely into their hands.

142. Czech pilots of No 310 Squadron (an all Czech Squadron) scramble at Dyce aerodrome near Aberdeen.

IN AID
OF
CLYDESIDE DISTRESS FUND

POLISH ARMY CHOIR

GLASGOW, MAY 1941

ANTI-ITALIAN FEELING

Orgy of Window-Breaking and Looting in Edinburgh

CROWDS DEMONSTRATE IN OTHER CITIES

Big Round-Up of New Enemy Aliens Throughout Britain

Thousands of Italians throughout the country to-day awaited a Home Office decision on their position now that Mussolini has declared war. Scattered in little shops and businesses, which many of them have made

145. A German Heinkel bomber brought down in East Lothian.

146. The bodies of two German airmen lie in St Philip's Church, Portobello, October 1939.

147. Wreckage from a German raider shot down in the Forth is salvaged at Port Seton.

148. German prisoners of war on agricultural duties at Newtongrange, Midlothian.

149. Hitler's deputy, Rudolph Hess, stepped from the wreckage of this plane in Ayrshire on his ill-fated peace mission.

150. Crew of a German U-boat which surrendered at Dundee at the end of the war.

The War at Sea

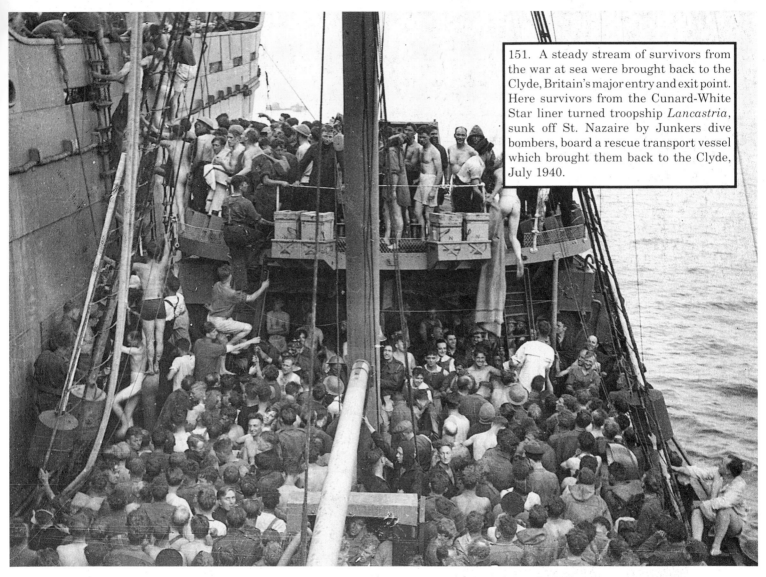

151. A steady stream of survivors from the war at sea were brought back to the Clyde, Britain's major entry and exit point. Here survivors from the Cunard-White Star liner turned troopship *Lancastria*, sunk off St. Nazaire by Junkers dive bombers, board a rescue transport vessel which brought them back to the Clyde, July 1940.

The training, preparation and organisation of the forces themselves spread throughout the country. Britain was like a giant aircraft carrier, anchored off hostile Europe, bristling with defences and simultaneously hurling attack after attack at the enemy across the Channel and the North Sea. Troops were everywhere in long convoys of trucks and bren gun carriers which churned fields and roads; section and platoon attacks were being rehearsed with murderous dedication in fields and mountains; villages were buzzed by high-spirited fighter pilots from above; mysterious explosions and strange cries in the night emitted from woods and glens; and there were even dark deeds being rehearsed on and below water in the sea lochs along the coastline.

More than 90 per cent of submarine crews were trained at Rothesay, where HMS *Cyclops* and the 7th Submarine Flotilla had been based from an early stage of the war. Operational duties were largely off France, but the main role was to train expertly and quickly. The crews of the midget submarines which successfully struck the *Tirpitz* in 1943 were trained entirely in Rothesay Bay and surrounding waters from HMS *Varbel*, which was requisitioned and renamed from the Kyles of Bute Hydropathic. All manner of amphibious training was carried out at beaches around Rosneath, which became a major US Naval base and funnel port. American battleships and carriers secretly fueled there and took on supplies and replacements.

Gareloch was one of the two most important top secret military ports during the war, the other being Cairnryan in the natural sea loch haven of Lochryan, near Stranraer. Both were opened after the fall of France in 1940 and, in the case of Gareloch, a Royal Engineer and Pioneer Corps army of 5,000 laid fifty miles of railtrack directly to six berths where twenty large cranes from Southampton Docks were quietly transferred, destination unknown. The first big ships berthed two years later. Both these ports were of vital importance in receiving and sending military equipment.

Gareloch serviced the biggest warships and HMS *Malay* even had new guns fitted there. Stranraer also swarmed with activity and there was a string of army camps like Aird, Bonniebraes, Drummuckloch, Leffnoll, Innermessan and the flying boat station at Wigg Bay to keep the seaway open and defended.

By far the largest airport development took place at Prestwick. Before the build-up to counter the German threat, Prestwick was little more than three farms and a clump of trees. After 1936 an RAF pilot and navigator training school was established and by the time the aerial Battle of Britain was fought 1,300 pilots had successfully passed through, many of whom were responsible for inflicting daunting losses on the *Luftwaffe*.

Even in 1939 Prestwick was hardly envisaged as a major base of the future but while America was still contemplating whether or not she would join in it was agreed that a supply of American-made planes would be delivered to us in support, routed from California to Canada then flying the Atlantic Ferry run to Britain.

The fact that they came to Prestwick at all was almost fortuitous. The receiving airport was RAF Aldergrove in Ireland, but on 29 November 1940 Captain E M Eaves, flying in with a Hudson, lost contact with the five other aircraft in the formation and landed by mistake at Prestwick. A year later it was the main reception airport and a new 300 feet wide by 6,600 feet long runway was built ready for the rush.

As the war progressed planes of all shapes and sizes arrived in such profusion and so fast that Prestwick just grew and grew to cope with the momentum. Lord Beaverbrook, the Press baron and a Canadian Scot who had been given responsibility for aircraft production, strove whip-in-hand for ever increasing delivery and expansion because he knew it was in this way that the war would be won. Wellingtons, Lancasters, Liberators, Spitfires, Hurricanes, Defiants, Beauforts and Hudsons all began to head for Prestwick. Six thousand bombers came winging out of the Atlantic on the Ferry run, on one occasion 350 in a single day and sometimes sixty aircraft in an hour.

After the long flight exhausted airmen would sleep before making their way to the Red Lion Hotel, which became the rendezvous point and the place to relax. American servicemen were everywhere looking for a good time and by the end of the war many Ayrshire girls had become GI Brides. In spite of the enormous activity, security remained a key priority and the scale of the great Prestwick airlift was never really understood. It was designated an international airport in 1945.

It was the Clyde, of course, that dominated the attention during the war. The role it played in ensuring victory can never be overestimated. It became a vital sea artery through which flowed all the essential elements of war: battleships used it as both haven and attack base; convoys mustered

153. Survivors of the *City of Benares* clamber aboard a warship.

152. *left:* Survivors of the *City of Benares* arrive at Greenock. The tragedy of this ship full of children — or "seavacs" as they were known — sunk in the Atlantic by a U-boat touched the hearts of the British public and led to a reversal of official policy on the evacuation of children.

"We were living in Newton Ayr at the time and my husband had a pass from Churchill Barracks which allowed him to join my son, daughter and myself in our digs. One night the siren went and he stood at the door in the darkness for quite a long time. When he came in he said that either there were German planes circling overhead or else it was waves of them coming in. Then the sky began to light up towards Glasgow. Of course, it was the first night of the Clydeside Blitz. Every time I hear a siren now my stomach still turns over."

Glasgow Pensioner

154. *above:* Convoys which formed the life blood of the country during the dark days of the war gathered at the Tail o' the Bank in the Clyde.

156. *right:* Captain Beaconsfield Worthington, master of the SS *Politician*, the famous *Whisky Galore* ship which grounded in the Hebrides and provided what has been called "the biggest free loading booze-bender of all time."

155. The *Empress of Britain* in the Clyde, 14 June 1940. She arrived in the company of the *Aquitania* (in the distance), *Empress of Canada* and the *Queen Mary* with the first contingent of Australian and New Zealand troops to arrive in Britain.

157. The cargo ship SS *Politician* pictured in ballast.

there before hazarding the U-boat gauntlet out across the Atlantic or to Russia; fighting ships and merchantmen were built there; even the Mulberry Harbours for the invasion to free Europe were constructed there. There were enormous movements of the traffic of war as men, guns, ammunition, machines and stores arrived and departed. Scotland was often the first sight incoming Commonwealth and American servicemen had of the European war theatre, and by the time peace was eventually won more than four million servicemen had either disembarked at or set out from the Clyde stronghold.

Apart from troop manoeuvres, shortages and family involvements in the services, large tracts of Scotland knew nothing of the Hot War, although the realities were stuck into the eye of Glasgow and the Clyde every day and every night. Many of the Home Front dramas took place on the Clyde where people were prepared for the best and the worst events at any time. It was from the Clyde that HMS *Hood*, the pride of the Royal Navy, sailed out to meet her death, leaving many Clydeside families who had made friends with the crew grieving at the devastating loss; it was into the Clyde that the battleship *Rodney*, the aircraft carrier *Victorious*, the cruiser *Norfolk* and a flotilla of destroyers returned triumphantly after the revenge sinking of the *Bismark* and the *Tirpitz* to be greeted by cheering crowds at the Tail o' the Bank. Many of the German survivors were landed as prisoners at Greenock and there were revealing and touching sights as some of the German wounded were helped with kindness by British troops while their more mobile comrades were marched off at bayonet point.

After the early tragedy of the *Athenia*, the Clyde witnessed the nightmares of sea warfare at its most ruthless as a sad trail of ravaged ships and their survivors were brought home. They arrived amidst tales of horror, heroism, dedication to duty, acts of naval professionalism and compassion: the blazing oil tanker *San Demetrio*; the sunken evacuee ships *City of Simla* and *Volendam*; the *City of Benares*, torpedoed four days into the Atlantic carrying some of the survivors from the *Volendam*; the *Empress of Britain*, torpedoed and dive-bombed off Ireland; the survivors from the sinking of the *Lancastria* off St Nazaire, the worst sea disaster of the war; the extraordinary seamanship of Captain Small, master of the *Imperial Transport*, who guided his ship home with the aid of a sixpenny atlas to run aground at Kilchattan Bay after being torpedoed 300 miles into the Atlantic; the sinking of the French battleship *Maille Breze* in Greenock harbour; the unexpected feast of fresh oranges and marmalade at Hunter's Quay after the *Empire Haywood Stanhope* was sabotaged by enemy agents in Spain on its passage from Seville to the Clyde; the direct hit on HMS *Sussex* in Yorkhill Basin; and the disaster of HMS *Curacao* struck amidships by the *Queen Mary*, whom she was escorting in her role of troopship making for the Clyde.

The *Queen Mary* and *Queen Elizabeth*, those famous Clyde-built sisters, were regular callers, transporting up to 15,000 servicemen at a time. Even some of the old Clyde steamers also played their part, particularly in the evacuation of Dunkirk, several becoming casualties, such as the *Eagle*

158. HMS *Cossack* enters Leith Harbour with merchant seamen dramatically rescued from the Nazi prison ship *Altmark* in a Norwegian Fjord. The action caused an international diplomatic furore but met with the wholehearted approval of the British people.

159. An early reverse was the sinking of the battleship *Royal Oak* in Scapa Flow in October 1939. Not only were more than 800 lives lost but the myth of the impregnability of the Royal Navy's northern anchorage was also exploded. It was a devastating blow to British morale.

160. Families of sailors aboard the *Royal Oak* scan the lists of survivors.

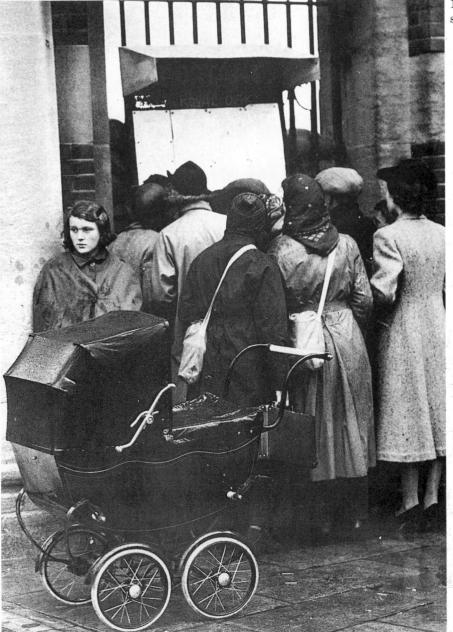

"I remember being home on leave in Greenock and seeing a British sailor making his way along the street as if he were sleep walking. As I drew level I saw the tears streaming down his cheeks. It was always difficult to know how to handle personal grief during the war and sometimes it was best to say nothing. However, on this occasion the sailor looked so downcast that involuntarily I asked him if he was okay. His reply, in broadest Cockney, shook me: 'The 'ood's dahn, mate', he said. 'The 'ood's dahn.' It was unbelievable. HMS *Hood*, the pride of the Navy, was sunk."

Former Naval Officer

161. A captured German U-boat tied up at the dockside, Leith.

162. The end of the war and a German minesweeper surrenders in the Forth, May 1945.

III, *Juno*, *Kylemore*, *Marmion*, *Mercury* and the *Waverley*. Below its air shield of barrage balloons, a boom was stretched between The Cloch and Dunoon, virtually impregnable to marauding U-boats. Indeed it was never breached during the whole war, although several U-boats were destroyed in the Clyde approaches. After one raid the bodies of twenty-six German submariners were found and buried in Greenock cemetery.

There was one scare in the dead of night that had Clydesiders leaping from their beds: it was believed that an enemy submarine had penetrated the boom and there was wild activity with depth charges exploding and searchlights playing on the waters as a frantic find-and-destroy hunt was mounted. The incident gave Goebbels, Hitler's director of propaganda, the opportunity to refer to it disparagingly in a German broadcast. It set minds wondering how he could have known about the incident so quickly and what kind of spy network could be operating on the Clyde.

The details of a spy ring were unknown, although it was understood that information about the activity on the Clyde could be of paramount importance to Germany. Strict security operated throughout the Firth, but for the trained agent there were easy leads to follow. A number of shops, for example, always had advance warning when various ships were arriving so that fresh stores would be available, especially fruit and vegetables, and newspaper parcels were often dumped on Greenock station platform addressed to specific battleships. Britain, for good reason, had a preoccupation with spies during the war and the poster campaign about loose talk costing lives was sound advice.

One of the few recorded cases of a spy being caught in the act in Scotland took place on the Clyde when Detective Inspector George Coupar and Sergeant Mort of Greenock police made the arrest in June 1941. The suspect claimed he had escaped from France and was accepted by the Free French Naval Headquarters in Greenock, then commissioned and used as an interpreter. When the police moved in he made a dash for his bedroom, but the inspector reached it first and found a British naval paybook complete with photograph and the forged signature of a British naval commander. On his way to Leeds Prison it is said the prisoner kept asking what was going to happen to him. The doughty police sergeant took out his warrant card and pointed to his name — Mort. The spy's fate is unrecorded.

163. East coast copastal shipping was under the constant threat of attack throughout the war. The little steamship *Highlander* was strafed by a German 'plane but succeeded in downing the attacker. Her plucky response to the attack caught the imagination of the public and war artist Sir Muirhead Bone made this drawing of the damaged ship.

164. *above:* The Commando Memorial at Spean Bridge.

165. *opposite page:* The 2nd Gordons in action at Nutterden, February 1945.

Front Line

During those early days of the war, Scotland may have received a hammering from the Germans but during all that time training was in progress to take the offensive to the enemy in a number of different ways. In the wake of Dunkirk it became clear that a hard-striking force of specially trained and highly motivated men capable of acting independently and expertly, who were masters of sabotage, mayhem and general skulduggery, was needed quickly. The 'rough bounds' of Knoydart, Moidart and Glenelg was the perfect training ground, and it was in this wild area of mountains, moors and sea lochs that rehearsals for the real thing began under officers from Scottish regiments and Scottish NCOs, with expert advice on the art of ground cover

and silent movement provided by stalkers from Lord Lovat's 'Scouts'.

The clans gathered. The first of the raw material consisted of 2,000 infantrymen recently returned from Norway, forced to sleep rough at the outset simply because there was no immediate accommodation available but kept wonderfully alert by the attentions of that prodigious army of man-eaters, the West Highland midge, its hunger sharpened in the warm weather. Given the task and knowing the desperate situations that would face their charges, the officers threw themselves into the training with fiendish enthusiasm. The first Commanding Officer was Colonel Brian Mayfield of the Scots Guards; he was joined by two other Scots Guards, Bill and David Stirling of Keir, cousins of Lord Lovat, who later developed reputations for their work and courage behind enemy lines in North Africa. Polar explorers Freddie Chapman, of the Seaforth Highlanders, and Martin Lindsay, of the Gordons, were also added to the team. There was also Everest climber Jim Gavin, a creative artist with booby traps, and the Adjutant was David Stacey, later replaced by Donald Gilchrist, from Paisley.

At the commencement of this very special training school, originally centred on Inverailort but covering an area that included the estates of Arisaig, Achterlew, Glenfinnan and Achnacarry, work began in independent companies, then as special service battalions and later as Commandos based at Achnacarry Castle, the home of Lochiel, Clan Chief of the Camerons. The new 'chief' in charge of Castle Commando, as it became known, was the redoubtable Lieutenant-Colonel Charles Edward Vaughan: tough, motivated, the born soldier who had made his way up through the ranks in the Coldstream Guards before transferring to the Buffs as RSM. He was then recalled from retirement in 1940 and commissioned. Later he was hailed the "Rommel of the North" complete with Cockney accent

Although such a devil-may-care outfit was regarded with suspicion by other branches of the forces, it immediately caught Churchill's imagination and he gave it his full blessing. In addition to the team's original array of talents, two Shanghai policemen who knew a thing or two about using a knife at close quarters or quick, silent death by throttling were soon enlisted. Along with those knowledgeable about safecracking, making mimic birdcalls and even Indian smoke signals, there were rock climbers, canoeists, and even dieticians who could advise on edible roots, fungi and worms so that the Commandos could survive off the land. Not that they were inhibited or without highly creative skills of their own in living off that rugged but bountiful knuckle of Scotland — salmon, sea trout and venison in or out of season appeared not infrequently on unofficial personal diet lists. Then they began training.

The Commando training based on Achnacarry Castle is legendary. The men were put through a gruelling ordeal of physical endurance in all weathers, including the worst of deep-freeze mountain-top winters, up frozen rock faces, dragging themselves through snowdrifts and iced torrents merely to survive the night in the comfort of another snowdrift. It bordered on torture and the insane, but it also forged an extraordinary and incomparable fighting force of resourcefulness, determination and confidence: men of pride in their achievements, their supreme physical shape, their ability to withstand the severest mental and bodily stress and still continue to fight. They were the kind of men guaranteed to win advantages in tight corners and in the end win wars.

Many fell by the wayside during training, but those who passed and joined their parent units on the Firth of Clyde — at Ayr, Saltcoats, Fairlie and Irvine — or went for enhanced naval training on Arran or up at Lochfyne and Scapa Flow were recognised by the time the war reached its conclusion as having accomplished their task with distinction. It was the start of the Commando and special training units whose distant cousins played their vital roles most recently in the Falklands War, perhaps with more sophisticated equipment, but most certainly with men of the same breed. Essentially, they are trained winners.

Lord Lovat, the Fraser clan chief from Beauly in Invernesshire, who as head of his own regiment of Lovat Scouts and a wartime legend himself, particularly associated

166. The rough cairn at the head of Glenfeshie in the Cairngorms which was the site of the Highland Fieldcraft Training Centre in 1943-44.

167. Commando training chiefs at Achnacarry House: Colonel Vaughan
(left) and Lord Lovat.

with No 4 Commando, summed up that ferocious training in an article in the old *Weekly Scotsman* some years ago:

"All Commandos absorbed the mystery of toughness. They learned in the West Highlands that guts was not necessarily the ability to punch or kick or knife a man — any bully can do that after a few beers at a street corner. In a good soldier, and more especially in a good officer, toughness had to be a subjective state, an ability to challenge hardship, relish dangerous action, and scorn unequal odds, to wrench an ankle and keep going when all hope has gone; to climb at speed the last back-breaking hill; to sleep in wet clothes and live on cold 'compo' rations in the rain; to get the best out of weary and resentful men when one was oneself too tired to think; above all to understand the true meaning of comradeship."

It was not only the Commandos who were trained in that tough countryside. The SOE (Special Operations Executive), the cloak-and-dagger men who worked behind enemy lines, also began to teach their highly specialist line of business in the autumn of 1940. The idea was that with Europe overrun, something should be done to encourage resistance movements from within. So in that magnificent country of high tops, white sand, blue sea and mystical islands, SOE dedicated itself, using Arisaig House, looking out over Loch nan Uamh, as a base. The object was to instill in its willing pupils the required knowledge for the delicate operations of underground warfare, blowing up bridges, railway lines, power stations and even Germans whenever that possibility presented itself without the risk of capture.

The men who took this honours course in deception, destruction and revenge were often existing members of resistance teams, slipped quietly out of France, or from Czechoslovakia, Poland, Germany, Norway or Belgium, or they had a score to settle. Some had managed to make their way to Britain before war was declared and now wanted to return to fight in their own way; some were British with detailed knowledge of an occupied country or city; some had escaped the German advance; some volunteered from the other side of the world because they felt they could serve a purpose and their country needed them. All were dedicated men of cold courage and all were bilingual.

The Poles centred on Traigh House, opposite Rhum and Eigg. The Czechs were based at Camusdarroch and Garramore, and alternated with Dutch and French contingents. Inverie and Glaschoille, up Loch Nevis in Knoydart, hosted Belgians, Italians, Norwegians, and once

170. The British Expeditionary Force, Milebosche, June 1940. These soldiers of the 7th Argyll & Sutherland Highlanders were cut off by the Germans but succeeded in breaking out and rejoined the ill-fated 51st Highland Division on the River Bresle.

even a Chinaman. New academies opened at Rhubana and Meoble and generally that magnificent countryside became like Sauchiehall Street — but with a very different kind of activity. For obvious reasons all these teams had to be kept apart, but they made great friends with the local people and in spite of night-time explosions, groups of wild men suddenly bursting from cover with blood-chilling cries and screaming instructions in strange gibberish that was neither English nor Gaelic, the local folk hardly raised an eyebrow, apart from a smile or a wave and sometimes a bucket of haddies from the pier.

The role of SOE has been told many times before. It was a particularly dangerous task and for operatives who were caught it normally meant execution after harrowing interrogation. The training among those great Scottish mountains and seascapes became famous in certain circles and in 1942 two members of staff were seconded to help launch the OSS, the Office of Strategic Services. The Americans also sent men for training to return as instructors and pass on the lessons learned in the Scottish hills.

"There was this Scots sergeant who was completely unflappable. He was seconded to us for a few weeks in Belgium before Dunkirk. The only headdress he ever wore was his glengarry. We used to annoy him by calling it a Scottish cheesecutter. He used to say that he wanted the Germans to see it because then they would know what they were up against and that was an advantage to us. I was really pleased to see it myself on some hairy occasions. When he was around with his glengarry we felt safer. I bet he came through the war in one piece."
Former RASC Driver

171. Back again in Europe and on the advance this time. Men of the 51st Highland Division catch a lift towards Hertogenbosch on the Dutch/German border, October 1944.

172. The misconceived Arnhem action. This photograph shows a patrol led by Capt Ogilvie of the Glider Pilot Regiment. Ogilvie, it is recorded, landed in his kilt.

173. "S" Coy, 1st Btn The Scots Guards board the transport *Derbyshire* in Naples Harbour, January 1944, en route for Anzio.

174. In Italy, General Mark Clark presents the Silver Star to Lieut Col A D Malcolm of the Argyll & Sutherland Highlanders.

175. "S" Coy, 1st Btn, The Scots Guards at Monte Cassino.

176. Gordon Highlanders at Singapore, 1941. Prior to the invasion, officers listen to a talk on anti-tank methods.

177. A 1941 exercise on Singapore island. Argyll & Sutherland Highlanders round up "fifth columnists".

178. Germany, 1945. Scottish troops guard German prisoners being taken into custody aboard a commandeered Opel Blitz fire engine.

179. The band of the 10th Btn, Highland Light Infantry, 15th (Scottish) Division, march past the Divisional Commander, Maj Gen Barber, Mulmeese October 1944.

180. The Prime Minister watches the massed bands of the 51st Highland Division at Goch, March 1945.

181. Members of the BEF await evacuation at St. Malo, May 1940.

182. Royal Scot Sgt Harkness of Edinburgh pens a letter home, Moostdijk,
November 1944.

183. The crowds in Castle Street, Aberdeen, 19 August 1945. The Lord Provost surveys the scene from his balcony.

Victory!

184. Men and supplies for the liberation of Norway leave Leith Docks.

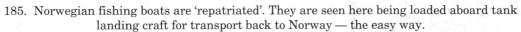

185. Norwegian fishing boats are 'repatriated'. They are seen here being loaded aboard tank landing craft for transport back to Norway — the easy way.

186. Demolition of the anti-tank defences on Aberdeen promenade, April 1946.

"I remember on VE night Glasgow went mad. There were parties everywhere, the flags were out and there was dancing on the streets. Everyone was laughing and singing and some were even crying. The drink was also flowing. I got very drunk and suddenly we all realised how much we wanted the war to be over."

Retired Glasgow Doctor

"Years after the war was over I was chatting to a group of young chaps in a pub. One of them said to me that he would quite like to have been in the war so long as he knew he was coming back. Well, that summed it all up, didn't it? I just said to him, 'Oh yes, sure, we all wished we knew we were coming back. But some didn't'."

Former Black Watch Corporal

187. VJ Day and dancing at the Ross Bandstand in Princes Street Gardens, Edinburgh.

188. The end of the war and the submarine HMS *Scotsman* returns to the harbour of Leith, May 1946.

SOURCES OF ILLUSTRATIONS

Scotsman: The Scotsman Publications Ltd, Edinburgh
IWM: The Imperial War Museum, London
EFS: Edinburgh Fire Service
Thomson: D C Thomson & Co Ltd, Dundee
Harris: Paul Harris, Whittingehame
Aberdeen: Aberdeen Journals Ltd
Huntly: Huntly House Museum, Edinburgh

1 Scotsman
2 Scotsman
3 Scotsman
4 Scotsman
5 Harris
6 IWM
7 IWM
8 IWM
9 IWM
10 IWM
11 Scotsman
12 IWM
13 Scotsman
14 Scotsman
15 Yorkshire Television
16 Thomson
17 Aberdeen
18 Scotsman
19 Huntly
20 Scotsman
21 Scotsman
22 Scotsman
23 Scotsman
24 Harris
25 EFS
26 Edinburgh ARP Guide
27 EFS
28 Edinburgh ARP Guide
29 Edinburgh ARP Guide
30 EFS
31 EFS
32 EFS
33 EFS
34 EFS
35 EFS
36 EFS
37 EFS
38 EFS
39 EFS
40 EFS
41 Harris
42 Harris
43 Museum of Transport, Glasgow
44 EFS/Firemen at War
45 EFS
46 EFS
47 Scotsman
48 Scotsman
49 EFS/Fireman at War
50 EFS/Fireman at War
51 Scotsman
52 Scotsman
53 Scotsman
54 Scotsman
55 Edinburgh ARP Guide
56 Scotsman
57 Scotsman

58 IWM
59 Aberdeen
60 Scottish National Portrait Gallery
61 Scotsman
62 Private Collection
63 Scotsman
64 Huntly
65 Scotsman
66 Scotsman
67 Scotsman
68 Scotsman
69 603 Squadron archives
70 Scotsman
71 Harris
72 Scotsman
73 Scotsman
73 Scotsman
74 Scotsman
75 Scotsman
76 Scotsman
77 EFS
78 Scotsman
79 Scotsman
80 Scotsman
81 Archive Picture
82 EFS/Firemen at War
83 Archive Picture
84 Harris
85 Archive Picture
86 Harris
87 Thomson
88 Harris
89 Thomson
90 Aberdeen
91 Aberdeen
92 EFS
93 Aberdeen
94 Aberdeen
95 Aberdeen
96 Scotsman
97 Scotsman
98 Museum of Transport, Glasgow
99 Scotsman
100 Museum of Transport, Glasgow
101 Scotsman
102 Scotsman
103 Scotsman
104 Huntly House
105 Aberdeen
106 Rolls Royce/Harris
107 Rolls Royce/Harris
108 Private collection
109 Thomson
110 Scotsman
111 Neil Morris
112 Huntly
113 North British Locomotive Co archives
114 North British Locomotive Co archives
115 Huntly
116 Scotsman
117 Scotsman
118 Thomson
119 Scotsman
120 Scotsman
121 Thomson
122 Thomson
123 Huntly
124 Scotsman
125 Scotsman
126 Harris
127 Scotsman

128 IWM
129 Scotsman
130 EFS
131 IWM
132 IWM
133 IWM
134 IWM
135 IWM
136 Thomson
137 Scotsman
138 IWM
139 Thomson
140 Harris
141 Harris
142 Aberdeen
143 Harris
144 Scotsman
145 Scotsman
146 Scotsman
147 Scotsman
148 Scotsman
149 Official photograph
150 Thomson
151 Harris/official photograph
152 Scotsman
153 Scotsman
154 Norman Burniston, Greenock
155 IWM
156 Solo Syndication
157 Solo Syndication
158 Scotsman
159 IWM
160 IWM
161 Scotsman
162 Scotsman
163 Archive
164 Hamish Campbell
165 IWM
166 Ian Nimmo
167 Ian Nimmo
168 Ian Nimmo
169 IWM
170 IWM
171 IWM
172 IWM
173 IWM
174 IWM
175 IWM
176 IWM
177 IWM
178 IWM
179 IWM
180 IWM
181 IWM
182 IWM
183 Aberdeen
184 Scotsman
185 Aberdeen
186 Aberdeen
187 Scotsman
188 Scotsman

Front cover: oil painting Rescue Party, Maryhill tenement, Kilmun Street, 14 March 1941 by Ian Fleming reproduced courtesy Paul Harris.
Back cover: Convoy Gathering, Gareloch by Alexander Nisbet Paterson reproduced courtesy The Fine Art Society Ltd.